MW01283203

THE RA MATERIAL

The Law of One
Book IV

The Law of One
Book IV

DON ELKINS CARLA RUECKERT
JAMES ALLEN McCARTY

REDFeather™

MIND | BODY | SPIRIT

4880 Lower Valley Road, Atglen, PA 19310

First Printing 1983
ISBN: 978-0-924608-10-0

*3,000 copies of The Law of One were privately printed by L/L Research, Louisville, KY, before it was printed under the title *The Ra Material*.

Type set in Chaparral Pro

Book IV
Softcover ISBN: 978-0-924608-10-0
Hardcover ISBN: 978-0-7643-6557-7
Box Set ISBN (Books I–V): 978-0-7643-6021-3
E-Book ISBN: 978-1-5073-0118-0

Printed in India

Updated Edition
10 9 8 7 6 5 4 3 2

Published by Red Feather Mind, Body, Spirit
An imprint of Schiffer Publishing, Ltd.
4880 Lower Valley Road
Atglen, PA 19310
Phone: (610) 593–1777; Fax: (610) 593–2002
E-mail: Info@schifferbooks.com
Web: www.redfeathermbs.com

For our complete selection of fine books on this and related subjects, please visit our website at www.schifferbooks.com. You may also write for a free catalog.

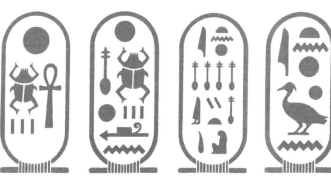

FOREWORD

On January 15, 1981, our research group started receiving a communication from the social memory complex Ra. From this communication precipitated the Law of One and some of the distortions of the Law of One.

The pages of this book contain an exact transcript, edited only to remove some personal material, of the communications received in Sessions 76 through 103 with Ra.

To a certain extent, this material presupposes a point of view that we have developed in the course of many years' study of the UFO phenomenon. If you are not familiar with our previous work, a reading of our book *Secrets of the UFO* might prove helpful in understanding the present material. Also, as you can see from this book's title, there are seventy-five previous sessions with Ra, which were collected in *The Law of One*, Books I, II, and III. If at all possible, it is good to begin with the beginning of this material, as later concepts build upon previous concepts. All these volumes are available from us by mail.

Those who gained familiarity with *The Law of One* through the mass-market publication of that volume under the title, *The Ra Material,* may be assured that the substantial introduction contained in that volume duplicates the subject matter contained in *Secrets of the UFO*, although *Secrets of the UFO* may still be interesting to you.

Book IV of *The Law of One* is a beginning in the examination of the nature and the proper metaphysical use of the archetypical mind. The archetypical mind is the mind of the Logos, the blueprint used to make the creation and the means by which we evolve in mind, body, and spirit. Ra stated that the archetypical mind could best be studied by one of three methods: the Tarot, astrology, or the Tree of Life, which is also known as white ceremonial magic. We decided to investigate the archetypical mind by delving into the Tarot, more especially the twenty-two images of the Major Arcana. In Book IV we work primarily with the first seven cards, which are archetypes for the structure of the mind. An overview of all the Tarot's twenty-two archetypes is also sought.

Any sensible consideration of a contact such as this would yield the conclusion that if the contact were valid, we would at some point begin receiving material the complete basis of which was not familiar to us. This has happened in Book IV. As you may see in the questioning, we scrambled as best we could throughout the entire volume in an attempt to keep up with the information that we were receiving, and to formulate reasonable questions. Even though our session schedule was relaxed, and the intervening time was used for study, we are aware that the questioning in this volume is more scattered than in the first three volumes of Ra sessions. We know of no solution to our own lack of knowledge and are at least confident that we cannot outdistance the reader, for we knew no more than you before we asked each question!

We do feel that it would be helpful if we included some information about the Tarot and its general terminology and compared that with a general outline of the Tarot from Ra's viewpoint, the viewpoint that Ra shared with the Egyptians so many years ago. The following comparison deals only with the twenty-two Major Arcana, since it was only these "concept complexes" that were used by Ra and that were later drawn by Egyptian priests, to describe the process of the evolution of the mind, the body, and the spirit. The Court Arcana and the Minor Arcana were of other influences and were concerned primarily with the astrological approach to this study. Each card is described first by its Arcanum number, then by traditional terminology, and third by Ra's terminology.

The cards upon which we originally questioned were not available for reprinting, so we have reproduced here the Major Arcana of the deck most closely resembling our first deck. These images are to be found in George Fathman's *The Royal Road: A Study in the Egyptian Tarot; Key to Sacred Numbers and Symbols* (Eagle Point, OR: Life Research Foundation, 1951).

As you can see, the first seven cards of the Major Arcana were designed to describe the evolution of the mind; the second seven, the evolution of the body; and the third seven, the evolution of the spirit. Arcanum Number XXII is called The Choice, and the choice spoken of is the central choice each conscious seeker or adept makes as it strives to master the lessons of the third-density experience to seek in service to others or in service to self.

Arcanum Number I

The Magician

MATRIX OF THE MIND

Arcanum Number II

The High Priestess

POTENTIATOR OF THE MIND

Arcanum Number III

The Empress

CATALYST OF THE MIND

Arcanum Number IV

The Emperor

EXPERIENCE OF THE MIND

Arcanum Number V
The Hierophant
SIGNIFICATOR OF THE MIND

Arcanum Number VI
The Lovers or Two Paths
TRANSFORMATION OF THE MIND

Arcanum Number VII
The Chariot
GREAT WAY OF THE MIND

THE
MIND

Arcanum Number VIII

Justice or Balance

MATRIX OF THE BODY

Arcanum Number IX

Wisdom or the Sage

POTENTIATOR OF THE BODY

Arcanum Number X

Wheel of Fortune

CATALYST OF THE BODY

Arcanum Number XI

The Enchantress

EXPERIENCE OF THE BODY

Arcanum Number XII
The Hanged Man or Martyr
SIGNIFICATOR OF THE BODY

Arcanum Number XIII
Death
TRANSFORMATION OF THE BODY

Arcanum Number XIV
The Alchemist
GREAT WAY OF THE BODY

THE
BODY

Arcanum Number XV
The Devil
MATRIX OF THE SPIRIT

Arcanum Number XVI
Lightning Struck Tower
POTENTIATOR OF THE SPIRIT

Arcanum Number XVII
The Star or Hope
CATALYST OF THE SPIRIT

Arcanum Number XVIII
The Moon
EXPERIENCE OF THE SPIRIT

Arcanum Number XIX
The Sun
SIGNIFICATOR OF THE SPIRIT

Arcanum Number XX
Judgment
TRANSFORMATION OF THE SPIRIT

Arcanum Number XXI
The World
GREAT WAY OF THE SPIRIT

THE
SPIRIT

Arcanum Number XXII
The Fool,

THE CHOICE

One of the primary discoveries in Book IV is the concept and purpose of the "veil of forgetting" that exists between the conscious and unconscious minds in our current third-density experience. Third densities closer to the center of our galaxy apparently did not have such a veil and, therefore, did not forget any event in any incarnation. This condition simplified each entity's experience and also the nature of that archetypical mind. Readers, therefore, should be aware that the questioning focuses on both pre-veil and post-veiling experiences and the archetypical minds of both types of experience in order to get a better understanding of our current veiled experience in the third density of this octave of creation.

As a result of our questioning we have drawn our own images, the first seven of which may be found at the back of this volume.

The Ra contact continued for 106 sessions, which were printed into four books in *The Law of One* series. They are available at your local bookstore, from Schiffer Publishing, or from us. If you wish to receive our quarterly newsletter, in which the best of our current channeling is published, please request that you be put on our mailing list.

L/L Research
DON ELKINS
CARLA L. RUECKERT
JAMES A. MCCARTY

PO Box 5195
Louisville, KY 40255-0195
July 8, 1983

Session 76,
February 3, 1982

RA: I am Ra. I greet you in the love and in the light of the One Infinite Creator. We communicate now.

QUESTIONER: Could you first please give me an indication of the condition of the instrument?

RA: I am Ra. This instrument is in a state of physical-complex bankruptcy, which has existed for some of the measure you call time. The vital energies are normal, with a strong spiritual-complex counterpart and will lending substance to the mind/body/spirit-complex energy levels.

QUESTIONER: Will our continued communication with Ra be deleterious to the physical energies of the instrument?

RA: I am Ra. We may answer in two modes. Firstly, if the instrument were thusly dedicated to this use with no transfer of energy of physical-complex nature, it would begin to call upon the vital energy itself, and this, done in any substantive measure, is actively deleterious to a mind/body/spirit complex if that complex wishes further experience in the illusion which it now distorts.

Secondly, if care is taken, firstly, to monitor the outer parameters of the instrument, then to transfer physical energy by sexual transfer, by magical protection, and, lastly, by the energetic displacements of thought-forms energizing the instrument during contact, there is no difficulty in that there is no worsening of the instrument's mind/body/spirit-complex distortions of strength/weakness.

It is to be noted that the instrument, by dedicating itself to this service, attracts greetings of which you are aware. These are inconvenient but, with care taken, need not be lastingly deleterious either to the instrument or the contact.

QUESTIONER: Of the three things that you mentioned that we could do for the instrument's benefit, would you clarify the last one? I didn't quite understand what you meant.

RA: I am Ra. As the entity which you are allows its being to empathize with any other being, so then it may choose to share with the other-self those energies which may be salubrious to the other-self. The mechanism of these energy transfers is the thought or, more precisely, the thought-form, for any thought is a form or symbol or thing that is an object seen in time/space reference.

QUESTIONER: Has our use of the Banishing Ritual of the Lesser Pentagram been of any value, and what is its effect?

RA: I am Ra. This group's use of the Banishing Ritual of the Lesser Pentagram has been increasingly efficacious. Its effect is purification, cleansing, and protection of the place of working.

The efficacy of this ritual is only beginning to be, shall we say, at the lower limits of the truly magical. In doing the working, those aspiring to adepthood have done the equivalent of beginning the schoolwork, many grades ahead. For the intelligent student this is not to be discouraged; rather to be encouraged is the homework, the reading, the writing, the arithmetic, as you might metaphorically call the elementary steps towards the study of being. It is the being that informs the working, not the working that informs the being. Therefore, we may leave you to the work you have begun.

QUESTIONER: Would it be beneficial for us to perform the banishing ritual more in this room?

RA: I am Ra. It is beneficial to regularly work in this place.

QUESTIONER: I am sorry that we have had such a long delay between the last session and this one. It couldn't be helped, I guess. Could you please tell me the origin of the Tarot?

RA: I am Ra. The origin of this system of study and divination is two-fold: firstly, there is that influence which, coming in a distorted fashion from those who were priests attempting to teach the Law of One in Egypt, gave form to the understanding, if you will pardon the misnomer, which they had received. These forms were then made a regular portion of the learn/teachings of an initiate. The second influence is that of those entities in the lands you call Ur, Chaldea, and Mesopotamia, who, from old, had received the, shall we say, data for which they called having to do with the heavens. Thusly we find two methods of divination being melded into one, with uneven results; the, as you call it, astrology and the form being combined to suggest what you might call the correspondences which are typical of the distortions you may see as attempts to view archetypes.

QUESTIONER: Then am I correct in assuming that the priests of

Egypt, in attempting to convert knowledge that they had received initially from Ra into understandable symbology, constructed and initiated the concept of the Tarot? Is this correct?

RA: I am Ra. This is correct, with the addition of the Sumerian influence.

QUESTIONER: Were Ra's teachings focusing on the archetypes for this Logos and the methods of achieving a very close approach to the archetypical configuration? Is this correct?

RA: I am Ra. This is correct without being true. We, of Ra, are humble messengers of the Law of One. We seek to teach/learn this single law. During the space/time of the Egyptian teach/learning, we worked to bring the mind complex, the body complex, and the spirit complex into an initiated state in which the entity could contact intelligent energy and so become teach/learner itself so that healing and the fruits of study could be offered to all. The study of the roots of mind is a portion of the vivification of the mind complex, and, as we have noted, the thorough study of the portion of the roots of mind called archetypical is an interesting and necessary portion of the process as a whole.

QUESTIONER: Is there, in Ra's opinion, any present-day value for the use of the Tarot as an aid in the evolutionary process?

RA: I am Ra. We shall repeat information. It is appropriate to study one form of constructed and organized distortion of the archetypical mind in depth in order to arrive at the position of being able to become and to experience archetypes at will. You have three basic choices. You may choose astrology, the twelve signs, as you call these portions of your planet's energy web, and what has been called the ten planets. You may choose the Tarot with its twenty-two so-called Major Arcana. You may choose the study of the so-called Tree of Life with its ten Sephiroth and the twenty-two relationships between the stations.

It is well to investigate each discipline, not as a dilettante but as one who seeks the touchstone, one who wishes to feel the pull of the magnet. One of these studies will be more attractive to the seeker. Let the seeker, then, investigate the archetypical mind, using, basically, one of these three disciplines. After a period of study, the discipline mastered sufficiently, the seeker may then complete the more important step: that is, the moving beyond the written in order to express in an unique fashion its understanding, if you may again pardon the noun, of the archetypical mind.

QUESTIONER: Would I be correct in saying that the archetypes of this particular Logos are somewhat unique with respect to the rest of the creation? The systems of study that we have just talked about would not translate quickly or easily in other parts of the creation. This is a very difficult question to state. Could you clear that up for me?

RA: I am Ra. We may draw from the welter of statement which you offer the question we believe you ask. Please requestion if we have mistaken your query. The archetypical mind is that mind which is peculiar to the Logos under which influence you are at this space/time distorting your experiences. There is no other Logos the archetypical mind of which would be the same any more than the stars would appear the same from another planet in another galaxy. You may correctly infer that the closer Logoi are indeed closer in archetypes.

QUESTIONER: Since Ra evolved initially on Venus, Ra is of the same archetypical origin as that which we experience here. Is this correct?

RA: I am Ra. This is correct.

QUESTIONER: But I am assuming that the concepts of the Tarot and the magical concepts of the Tree of Life etc. were not in use by Ra. I suspect, possibly, some form of astrology was a previous Ra concept. This is just a guess. Am I correct?

RA: I am Ra. To express Ra's methods of study of the archetypical mind under the system of distortions which we enjoyed would be to skew your own judgment of that which is appropriate for the system of distortions forming the conditions in which you learn/teach. Therefore, we must invoke the Law of Confusion.

QUESTIONER: I am going to ask some questions now that may be a little off the center of what we are trying to do. I'm not sure, because I'm trying to, with these questions, unscramble something that I consider very basic to what we are doing. Please forgive my lack of ability in questioning, since this is a difficult concept for me.

Could you give me an idea of the length of the first and second densities as they occurred for this planet?

RA: I am Ra. There is no method of estimation of the time/space before timelessness gave way in your first density. To the beginnings of your time, the measurement would be vast, and yet this vastness is meaningless. Upon the entry into the constructed space/time, your first density spanned a bridge of space/time and time/space of perhaps two billion of your years.

Second density is more easily estimated and represents your longest density in terms of the span of space/time. We may estimate that time as approximately 4.6 billion years. These approximations are exceedingly rough due to the somewhat uneven development which is characteristic of creations which are built upon the foundation stone of free will.

QUESTIONER: Did you state that second density was 4.6 billion years? B, b-i-l? Is that correct?

RA: I am Ra. This is correct.

QUESTIONER: Then we have a third density that is, comparatively speaking, the twinkling of an eye, the snap of a finger in time compared to the others. Why is the third density cycled so extremely rapidly compared to the first and second?

RA: I am Ra. The third density is a choice.

QUESTIONER: Third density, then, compared to the rest of the densities, all of them, is nothing but a uniquely short period of what we consider to be time, and is for the purpose of this choice.
    Is this correct?

RA: I am Ra. This is precisely correct. The prelude to choice must encompass the laying of the foundation, the establishment of the illusion, and the viability of that which can be made spiritually viable. The remainder of the densities is continuous refining of the choice. This also is greatly lengthened, as you would use the term. The choice is, as you put it, the work of a moment but is the axis upon which the creation turns.

QUESTIONER: Is this third-density choice the same throughout all of the creation of which you are aware?

RA: I am Ra. We are aware of creations in which third density is lengthier and more space/time is given to the choosing. However, the proportions remain the same, the dimensions all being somewhat etiolated and weakened by the Logos to have a variant experience of the Creator. This creation is seen by us to be quite vivid.

QUESTIONER: I didn't understand what you meant by what you said "as seen by you to be quite vivid." What did you mean?

RA: I am Ra. This creation is somewhat more condensed by its Logos than some other Logoi have chosen. Thus each experience of the Creator by the Creator in this system of distortions is, relatively speaking, more bright or, as we said, vivid.

QUESTIONER: I am assuming that upon entry into third density, for this planet, disease did not exist in any form. Is this correct?

RA: I am Ra. This is incorrect.

QUESTIONER: What disease or form of disease was there, and why did this exist at the beginning of the third density?

RA: I am Ra. Firstly, that which you speak of as disease is a functional portion of the body complex which offers the body complex the opportunity to cease viability. This is a desirable body complex function. The second portion of the answer has to do with second-density other-selves of a microscopic, as you would call it, size which have in some forms long existed and perform their service by aiding the physical-body complex in its function of ceasing viability at the appropriate space/time.

QUESTIONER: What I am trying to understand is the difference between the plan of the Logos for these second-density entities and the generation of what I would guess to be more or less a runaway array of feedback to create various physical problems to act as catalyst in our present third-density condition. Could you give me an indication of whether my thinking is anywhere near right on that?

RA: I am Ra. This instrument's physical-body complex is becoming more distorted towards pain. We shall, therefore, speak to this subject as our last full query of this working. Your query contains some internal confusion which causes the answer to be perhaps more general than desired. We invite refinements of the query.

The Logos planned for entities of mind/body/spirit complex to gain experience until the amount of experience was sufficient for an incarnation. This varied only slightly from second-density entities, whose mind/body complexes existed for the purpose of experiencing growth and seeking consciousness. As the third density upon your planet proceeded, as has been discussed, the need for the physical-body complex to cease became more rapidly approached due to intensified and more rapidly gained catalyst. This catalyst was not being properly assimilated. Therefore, the, shall we say, lifetimes needed to be shorter that learning might continue to occur with the proper rhythm and increment. Thus, more and more opportunities have been offered as your density has progressed for disease. May we ask if there are further brief queries before we close?

QUESTIONER: I have one question that is possibly of no value. You don't have to expand on it, but there is a crystal skull in the possession of a woman near Toronto. It may be of some value in investigating these communications with Ra, since I think possibly this had some origin from Ra. Can you tell me anything about that, and then is there anything that we can do to improve the contact or to make the instrument more comfortable?

RA: I am Ra. Although your query is one which uncovers interesting material, we cannot answer due to the potential an answer may have for affecting your actions. The appurtenances are carefully placed and requisite care taken. We are appreciative. All is well.

I am Ra. I leave you, my friends, in the love and the light of the One Infinite Creator. Go forth, therefore, glorying and rejoicing in the power and in the peace of the One Infinite Creator. Adonai.

Session 77,
February 10, 1982

RA: I am Ra. I greet you in the love and in the light of the One Infinite Creator. We communicate now.

QUESTIONER: Could you please give me an indication of the condition of the instrument?

RA: I am Ra. It is as previously stated.

QUESTIONER: Was the instrument under attack just prior to this session?

RA: I am Ra. This is correct.

QUESTIONER: Is there anything that we could do to help protect the instrument from these attacks prior to the session?

RA: I am Ra. This is correct.

QUESTIONER: What could we do?

RA: I am Ra. Your group could refrain from continuing this contact.

QUESTIONER: Is that the only thing that we could do?

RA: I am Ra. That is the only thing you could do which you are not already attempting with a whole heart.

QUESTIONER: I have three questions that the instrument asked me to ask, which I will get out of the way first. She wants to know if the preparation for her hospital experience could be improved if she should ever have to repeat it.

RA: I am Ra. All was done well with one exception. The instrument was instructed to spend space/time contemplating itself as the Creator. This, done in a more determined fashion, would be beneficial at times when the mind complex is weakened by severe assaults upon the distortions of the body complex towards pain. There is no necessity for negative thought-forms regardless of pain distortions. The elimination of such creates the lack of possibility for negative elementals and other negative entities to use these thought-forms to create the worsening of the mind-complex deviation from the normal distortions of cheerfulness/anxiety.

QUESTIONER: The instrument would also like to know if what we call tuning could be improved during times when we do not communicate with Ra.

RA: I am Ra. That which has been stated in regard to the latter question will suffice to point the way for the present query.

QUESTIONER: Finally, she wishes to know why several days ago her heart rate went up to 115 per minute, and why she had extreme pain in her stomach. Was that an Orion greeting?

RA: I am Ra. Although this experience was energized by the Orion group, the events mentioned, as well as others more serious, were proximally caused by the ingestion of certain foodstuffs in what you call your tablet form.

QUESTIONER: Can you tell me what these tablets were, specifically?

RA: I am Ra. We examine this query for the Law of Confusion and find ourselves close to the boundary, but acceptably so.

The substance which caused the bodily reaction of the heartbeat was called Pituitone by those which manufacture it. That which caused the difficulty which seemed to be cramping of the lower abdominal musculature but was, in fact, more organic in nature was a substance called Spleentone.

This instrument has a physical-body complex of complicated balances which afford it physical existence. Were the view taken that certain functions and chemicals found in the healthy, as you call it, body complex are lacking in this one and, therefore, simply must be replenished, the intake of the many substances which this instrument began would be appropriate. However, this particular physical vehicle has, for approximately twenty-five of your years, been vital due to the spirit, the mind, and the will being harmoniously dedicated to fulfilling the service it chose to offer.

Therefore, physical healing techniques are inappropriate whereas mental and spiritual healing techniques are beneficial.

QUESTIONER: Is there any technique that we could use that we have not been using that would be beneficial for the instrument in this case?

RA: I am Ra. We might suggest, without facetiousness, two.

Firstly, let the instrument remove the possibility of further ingestion of this group of foodstuffs.

Secondly, each of the group may become aware of the will to a greater extent. We cannot instruct upon this but merely indicate, as we have previously, that it is a vital key to the evolution of the mind/body/spirit complex.

QUESTIONER: Thank you. I would like to go back to the plan of this Logos for Its creation and examine the philosophical basis that is the foundation for what was created in this local creation and the philosophy of the plan for experience. I am assuming that I am correct in stating that the foundation for this, as has been stated many times before, is the first distortion. After that, what was the plan in the philosophical sense?

RA: I am Ra. We cannot reply due to a needed portion of your query which has been omitted; that is, do we speak of this particular Logos?

QUESTIONER: That is correct. I am asking with respect to this particular sub-Logos, our sun.

RA: I am Ra. This query has substance. We shall begin by turning to an observation of a series of concept complexes of which you are familiar as the Tarot.

The philosophy was to create a foundation, first of mind, then of body, and then of spiritual complex. Those concept complexes you call the Tarot lie then in three groups of seven: the mind cycle, one through seven; the physical-complex cycle, eight through fourteen; the spiritual-complex cycle, fifteen through twenty-one. The last concept complex may best be termed The Choice.

Upon the foundation of the transformation of each complex, with free will guided by the root concepts offered in these cycles, the Logos offered this density the basic architecture of a building and the constructing and synthesizing of data culminating in The Choice.

QUESTIONER: Then to condense your statement, I see it meaning that there are seven basic philosophical foundations for mental experience, seven for bodily, seven for spiritual, and that these produce the polarization that we experience sometime during the third-density cycle. Am I correct?

RA: I am Ra. You are correct in that you perceive the content of our prior statement with accuracy. You are incorrect in that you have no mention of the, shall we say, location of all of these concept complexes; that is, they exist within the roots of the mind, and it is from this resource that their guiding influence and leitmotifs[1] may be traced. You may further note that each foundation is itself not single but a complex of concepts. Furthermore, there are relationships betwixt mind, body, and spirit of the same location in octave, for instance: one, eight, fifteen, and relationships within each octave which are helpful in the pursuit of The Choice by the mind/body/spirit complex. The Logos under which these foundations stand is one of free will. Thusly the foundations may be seen to have unique facets and relationships for each mind/body/spirit complex. Only twenty-two, The Choice, is relatively fixed and single.

QUESTIONER: Then I am probably having a problem with the concept of time, since it appears that the Logos was aware of the polarization choice. It seems that this choice for polarization at the end of third

---

1. Leitmotif—Lit: Leading motive. In Music: A distinguishing theme or melodic phrase representing and recurring with a given character, situation, or emotion in an opera.

density is an important philosophical plan for the experience past third density. Am I correct in assuming that this process is a process to create the proper or desired experience that will take place in the creation after third density is complete?

RA: I am Ra. These philosophical foundations are those of third density. Above this density there remains the recognition of the architecture of the Logos, but without the veils which are so integral a part of the process of making the choice in third density.

QUESTIONER: The specific question that I had was that it seems to me that the choice was planned to create intense polarization past third density so that experience would be intense past third density. Is this correct?

RA: I am Ra. Given that our interpretation of your sound vibration complexes is appropriate, this is incorrect. The intensity of fourth density is that of the refining of the rough-hewn sculpture. This is, indeed, in its own way, quite intense, causing the mind/body/spirit complex to move ever inward and onward in its quest for fuller expression. However, in third density the statue is forged in the fire. This is a type of intensity which is not the property of fourth, fifth, sixth, or seventh densities.

QUESTIONER: What I am really attempting to understand, since all of these twenty-one philosophical bases result in the twenty-second, which is The Choice, is why this choice is so important, why the Logos seems to put so much emphasis on this choice, and what function this choice of polarity has, precisely, in the evolution or the experience of that which is created by the Logos?

RA: I am Ra. The polarization or choosing of each mind/body/spirit is necessary for harvestability from third density. The higher densities do their work due to the polarity gained in this choice.

QUESTIONER: Would it be possible for this work of our density to be performed if all of the sub-Logoi chose the same polarity in any particular expression or evolution of a Logos? Let us make the assumption that our sun created nothing but, through the first distortion, positive polarity. There was no product except positive polarity. Would work then be done in fourth density and higher as a function of only the positive polarization evolving from the original creation of our sub-Logos?

RA: I am Ra. Elements of this query illustrate the reason I was unable to answer your previous question without knowledge of the Logos involved. To turn to your question, there were Logoi which chose to set the plan for the activation of mind/body/spirit complexes through each true color body without recourse to the prior application of free will. It is, to our knowledge, only in an absence of free will that the conditions of which you speak obtain. In such a procession of densities, you find an extraordinarily long, as you measure time, third density; likewise, fourth density. Then, as the entities begin to see the Creator, there is a very rapid, as you measure time, procession towards the eighth density. This is due to the fact that one who knows not, cares not.

Let us illustrate by observing the relative harmony and unchanging quality of existence in one of your, as you call it, primitive tribes. The entities have the concepts of lawful and taboo, but the law is inexorable and all events occur as predestined. There is no concept of right and wrong, good or bad. It is a culture in monochrome. In this context you may see the one you call Lucifer as the true light-bringer in that the knowledge of good and evil both precipitated the mind/body/spirits of this Logos from the Edenic conditions of constant contentment and also provided the impetus to move, to work, and to learn.

Those Logoi whose creations have been set up without free will have not, in the feeling of those Logoi, given the Creator the quality and variety of experience of Itself as have those Logoi which have incorporated free will as paramount. Thusly you find those Logoi moving through the timeless states at what you would see as a later space/time to choose the free-will character when elucidating the foundations of each Logos.

QUESTIONER: I guess, under the first distortion, it was the free will of the Logos to choose to evolve without free will. Is this correct?

RA: I am Ra. This is correct.

QUESTIONER: Do the Logoi that choose this type of evolution choose both the service-to-self and the service-to-others path for different Logoi, or do they choose just one of the paths?

RA: I am Ra. Those, what you would call, early Logoi, which chose lack of free-will foundations, to all extents with no exceptions, founded Logoi of the service-to-others path. The, shall we say, saga of polarity, its consequences and limits, were unimagined until experienced.

QUESTIONER: In other words, you are saying that originally the Logoi that did not choose this free-will path did not choose it simply because they had not conceived of it, and that later Logoi, extending the first distortion farther down through their evolution, experienced it as an outcropping or growth from that extension of the first distortion. Am I correct in saying that?

RA: I am Ra. Yes.

QUESTIONER: Then did this particular Logos that we experience plan for this polarity and know all about it prior to Its plan? I suspect that this is what happened.

RA: I am Ra. This is quite correct.

QUESTIONER: In that case, as a Logos, you would have an advantage of selecting the form of acceleration, you might say, of spiritual evolution by planning what we call the major archetypical philosophical foundations and planning these as a function of the polarity that would be gained in third density. Is this correct?

RA: I am Ra. This is exquisitely correct.

QUESTIONER: In that case, it seems that a thorough knowledge of the precise nature of these philosophical foundations would be of primary importance to the study of evolution of mind, body, and spirit, and I would like to carefully go through each, starting with the mind. Is this agreeable with Ra?

RA: I am Ra. This is agreeable with two requests which must be made. Firstly, that an attempt be made to state the student's grasp of each archetype. We may then comment. We cannot teach/learn to the extent of learn/teaching. Secondly, we request that it be constantly kept before the mind, as the candle before the eye, that each mind/body/spirit complex shall and should and, indeed, must perceive each archetype, if you use this convenient term, in its own way. Therefore, you may see that precision is not the goal; rather, the quality of general-concept complex perception is the goal.

QUESTIONER: Now, there are several general concepts that I would like to be sure that we have clear before going into this process, and I will certainly adhere to the requests that you have just stated.

When our Logos designed this particular evolution of experience, It decided to use a system of which we spoke, allowing for polarization through total free will. How is this different from the Logos that does not do this? I see the Logos creating the possibility of increase in vibration through the densities. How are the densities provided for and set by the Logos, if you can answer this?

RA: I am Ra. This shall be the last full query of this working. The psychic attack upon this instrument has, shall we say, left scars which must be tended, in our own opinion, in order to maintain the instrument.

Let us observe your second density. Many come more rapidly to third density than others, not because of an innate efficiency of catalysis but because of unusual opportunities for investment. In just such a way those of fourth density may invest third, those of fifth density may invest fourth. When fifth density has been obtained, the process takes upon itself a momentum based upon the characteristics of wisdom when applied to circumstance. The Logos Itself, then, in these instances provides investment opportunities, if you wish to use that term. May we inquire if there are any brief queries at this space/time?

QUESTIONER: Is there anything that we can do after this contact to increase the comfort as related to the psychic attack, or is there anything that we can do to make the instrument more comfortable and to improve the contact in the present situation?

RA: I am Ra. The faculties of healing which each has commenced energizing may be used. The entity may be encouraged to remain motionless for a period. As it will not appreciate this, we suggest the proper discussion.

The physical appurtenance called the censer was just a degree off, this having no deeper meaning. We do ask, for reasons having to do with the physical comfort of the instrument, that you continue in your careful efforts at alignment. You are conscientious. All is well.

We leave you, my friends, in the glorious love and light of the One Creator. Go forth, therefore, rejoicing in the power and in the peace of the One Infinite Creator. I am Ra. Adonai.

Session 78,
February 19, 1982

RA: I am Ra. I greet you in the love and in the light of the One Infinite Creator. We communicate now.

QUESTIONER: Was there some problem with the ritual we performed that made it necessary to perform the ritual twice?

RA: I am Ra. There was a misstep which created a momentary lapse of concentration. This was not well.

QUESTIONER: What was the misstep?

RA: I am Ra. It was a missed footing.

QUESTIONER: Did this have any detrimental effect on the instrument?

RA: I am Ra. Very little. The instrument felt the presence it has come to associate with cold and spoke. The instrument did the appropriate thing.

QUESTIONER: Could you tell me the condition of the instrument?

RA: I am Ra. The physical complex is as previously stated. There is some slight loss of vital energy. The basic complex distortions are similar to your previous asking.

QUESTIONER: The instrument would like for me to ask if there is any problem with her kidneys.

RA: I am Ra. This query is more complex than its brevity certifies. The physical-complex renal system of this instrument is much damaged. The time/space equivalent which rules the body complex is without flaw. There was a serious question, due to psychic attack, as to whether the spiritual healing of this system would endure. It did so but has the need to be reinforced by affirmation of the ascendancy of the spiritual over the apparent or visible.

When this instrument began ingesting substances designed to heal in a physical sense, among other things, the renal complex, this instrument was ceasing the affirmation of healing. Due to this, again, the healing was weakened. This is of some profound distortion, and it would be well for the instrument to absorb these concepts. We ask your forgiveness for offering information which may abridge free will, but the dedication of the instrument is such that it would persevere regardless of its condition, if possible. Thusly we offer this information that it may persevere with a fuller distortion towards comfort.

QUESTIONER: What was the experience that caused the healing of the time/space kidney?

RA: I am Ra. This experience was the healing of self by self with the catalyst of the spiritual healer whom you call Pachita.

QUESTIONER: Thank you. In utilizing the energetic displacements of thought-forms energizing the instrument during contact most efficiently, what specifically could we do?

RA: I am Ra. Each of the support group has an excess of love and light to offer the instrument during the working. Already each sends to the instrument love, light, and thoughts of strength of the physical, mental, and spiritual configurations. These sendings are forms. You may refine these sendings until the fullest manifestations of love and light are sent into the energy web of this entity which functions as instrument. Your exact sending is, in order to be most potent, the creature of your own making.

QUESTIONER: Thank you. I am going to go back to an earlier time, if you could call it that, in evolution to try to establish a very fundamental base for some of the concepts that seem to be the foundation of everything that we experience so that we can more fully examine the basis of our evolution.

I am guessing that in our Milky Way galaxy (the major galaxy with billions of stars) that the progress of evolution was from the center outward toward the rim, and that in the early evolution of this galaxy, the first distortion was not extended down past the sub-Logos simply because it was not thought of or conceived of, and that this extension of the first distortion, which created polarization, was something that occurred in what we would call a later time as the evolution progressed outward from the center of the galaxy. Am I in any way correct in this statement?

RA: I am Ra. You are correct.

QUESTIONER: We have the first, second, and third distortions of the

Law of One as free will, love, and light. Am I correct in assuming that the central core of this major galaxy began to form with the third distortion? Was that the origin of our Milky Way galaxy?

RA: I am Ra. In the most basic or teleological sense you are incorrect, as the One Infinite Creator is all that there is. In an undistorted seed form, you are correct in seeing the first manifestation visible to the eye of the body complex which you inhabit as the third distortion, light, or to use a technical term, limitless light.

QUESTIONER: I realize that we are on very difficult ground, you might say, for precise terminology. It is totally displaced from our system of coordinates for evaluation in our present system of language.

These early Logoi that formed in the center of the galaxy wished, I assume, to create a system of experience for the One Creator. Did they then start with no previous experience or information about how to do this? This is difficult to ask.

RA: I am Ra. At the beginning of this creation or, as you may call it, octave, there were those things known which were the harvest of the preceding octave. About the preceding creation, we know as little as we do of the octave to come. However, we are aware of those pieces of gathered concept which were the tools which the Creator had in the knowing of the self.

These tools were of three kinds. Firstly, there was an awareness of the efficiency for experience of mind, body, and spirit. Secondly, there was an awareness of the most efficacious nature or, if you will, significator of mind, body, and spirit. Thirdly, there was the awareness of two aspects of mind, of body, and of spirit that the significator could use to balance all catalyst. You may call these two the matrix and the potentiator.

QUESTIONER: Could you elaborate please on the nature and quality of the matrix and the potentiator?

RA: I am Ra. In the mind complex the matrix may be described as consciousness. It has been called the Magician. It is to be noted that of itself, consciousness is unmoved. The potentiator of consciousness is the unconscious. This encompasses a vast realm of potential in the mind.

In the body the matrix may be seen as Balanced Working or Even Functioning. Note that here the matrix is always active, with no means of being inactive. The potentiator of the body complex, then, may be called Wisdom, for it is only through judgment that the unceasing activities and proclivities of the body complex may be experienced in useful modes.

The Matrix of the Spirit is what you may call the Night of the Soul or Primeval Darkness. Again we have that which is not capable of movement or work. The potential power of this extremely receptive matrix is such that the potentiator may be seen as Lightning. In your archetypical system called the Tarot, this has been refined into the concept complex of the Lightning Struck Tower. However, the original potentiator was light in its sudden and fiery form; that is, the lightning itself.

QUESTIONER: Would you elucidate with respect to the significator you spoke of?

RA: I am Ra. The original significators may undifferentiatedly be termed the mind, the body, and the spirit.

QUESTIONER: Then we have, at the beginning of this galactic evolution, an archetypical mind that is the product of the previous octave, which this galaxy then used as and acts upon under the first distortion so as to allow for what we experience as polarity. Was there any concept of polarity carried through from the previous octave in the sense of service-to-others or service-to-self polarity?

RA: I am Ra. There was polarity in the sense of the mover and the moved. There was no polarity in the sense of service to self and service to others.

QUESTIONER: Then the first experiences, as you say, were in monochrome. Was the concept of the seven densities of vibration with the evolutionary process taking place in discrete densities carried through from the previous octave?

RA: I am Ra. To the limits of our knowledge, which are narrow, the ways of the octave are without time; that is, there are seven densities in each creation infinitely.

QUESTIONER: Then I am assuming that the central suns of our galaxy, in starting the evolutionary process in this galaxy, provided for, in their plans, the refinement of consciousness through the densities just as we experience it here. However, they did not conceive of the polarization of consciousness with respect to service to self and service to others. Is this correct?

RA: I am Ra. This is correct.

QUESTIONER: Why do the densities have the qualities that they have? You have named the densities with respect to their qualities, the next density being that of love and so on. Can you tell me why these qualities exist in that form? Is it possible to answer that question?

RA: I am Ra. It is possible.

QUESTIONER: Will you please answer that?

RA: I am Ra. The nature of the vibratory range peculiar to each quantum of the octave is such that the characteristics of it may be described with the same certainty with which you perceive a color with your optical apparatus if it is functioning properly.

QUESTIONER: So the original evolution then was planned by the Logos, but the first distortion was not extended to the product. At some point this first distortion was extended and the first service-to-self polarity emerged. Is this correct, and, if so, could you tell me the history of this process of emergence?

RA: I am Ra. As proem, let me state that the Logoi always conceived of themselves as offering free will to the sub-Logoi in their care. The sub-Logoi had freedom to experience and experiment with consciousness, the experiences of the body, and the illumination of the spirit. That having been said, we shall speak to the point of your query.

The first Logos to instill what you now see as free will, in the full sense, in Its sub-Logoi came to this creation due to contemplation in depth of the concepts or possibilities of conceptualizations of what we have called the significators. The Logos posited the possibility of the mind, the body, and the spirit as being complex. In order for the significator to be what it is not, it then must be granted the free will of the Creator. This set in motion a quite lengthy, in your terms, series of Logos's improving or distilling this seed thought. The key was the significator becoming a complex.

QUESTIONER: Then our particular Logos, when it created Its own particular creation, was at some point far down the evolutionary spiral of the experiment, with the significator becoming what it was not and, therefore, I am assuming, was primarily concerned in designing the archetypes in such a way that they would create the acceleration of this polarization. Is this in any way correct?

RA: I am Ra. We would only comment briefly. It is generally correct. You may fruitfully view each Logos and Its design as the Creator experiencing Itself. The seed concept of the significator being a complex introduces two things: firstly, the Creator against Creator in one sub-Logos in what you may call dynamic tension; secondly, the concept of free will, once having been made fuller by its extension into the sub-Logoi known as mind/body/spirit complexes, creates and re-creates and continues to create as a function of its very nature.

QUESTIONER: You stated previously that The Choice is made in this third density and is the axis upon which the creation turns. Could you expand on your reason for making that statement?

RA: I am Ra. This is a statement of the nature of creation as we speak to you.

QUESTIONER: I did not understand that. Could you say that in a different way?

RA: I am Ra. As you have noted, the creation of which your Logos is a part is a protean entity which grows and learns upon a macrocosmic scale. The Logos is not a part of time. All that is learned from experience in an octave is, therefore, the harvest of that Logos and is further the nature of that Logos.

The original Logos's experience was, viewed in space/time, small; Its experience now, more. Therefore we say, as we now speak to you at this space/time, the nature of creation is as we have described. This does not deny the process by which this nature has been achieved, but merely ratifies the product.

QUESTIONER: After third density, in our experience, social memory complexes are polarized positively and negatively. Is the interaction of social memory complexes of opposite polarity equivalent, but on a magnified scale, to the interaction between mind/body/spirit complexes of opposite polarity? Is this how experience is gained as a function of polarity difference in fourth and fifth densities?

RA: I am Ra. No.

QUESTIONER: This is a hard question to ask, but what is the value experientially of the formation of positive and negative social memory complexes, of the separation of the polarities at that point rather than the allowing for the mixing of mind/body/spirit complexes of opposite polarity in the higher densities?

RA: I am Ra. The purpose of polarity is to develop the potential to do work. This is the great characteristic of those, shall we say, experiments which have evolved since the concept of The Choice was appreciated. Work is done far more efficiently and with greater purity, intensity, and variety by the voluntary searching of mind/body/spirit complexes for the lessons of third and fourth densities. The action of fifth density is viewed in space/time the same with or without polarity. However, viewed in time/space, the experiences of wisdom are greatly enlarged and deepened due, again, to the voluntary nature of polarized mind/body/spirit action.

QUESTIONER: Then you are saying that as a result of the polarization in consciousness, which has occurred later in the galactic evolution, the experiences are much more intense along the two paths. Are these experiences each independent of the other? Must there be action across the potentiated difference between the positive and negative polarity, or is it possible to have this experience simply because of the single polarity? This is difficult to ask.

RA: I am Ra. We would agree. We shall attempt to pluck the gist of your query from the surrounding verbiage.

The fourth and fifth densities are quite independent, the positive polarity functioning with no need of negative and vice versa. It is to be noted that in attempting to sway third-density mind/body/spirit complexes in choosing polarity, there evolves a good bit of interaction between the two polarities. In sixth density, the density of unity, the positive and negative paths must needs take in each other, for all now must be seen as love/light and light/love. This is not difficult for the positive polarity which sends love and light to all other-selves. It is difficult enough for service-to-self polarized entities that at some point the negative polarity is abandoned.

QUESTIONER: The choice of polarity being unique as a circumstance, shall I say, for the archetypical basis for the evolution of consciousness in our particular experience indicates to me that we have arrived, through a long process of the Creator knowing Itself, at a position of present or maximum efficiency for the design of a process of experience. That design for maximum efficiency is in the roots of consciousness and is the archetypical mind and is a product of everything that has gone before. There are, unquestionably, relatively pure archetypical concepts for the seven concepts for mind, body, and spirit. I feel that the language that we have for these is somewhat inadequate.

However, we shall continue to attempt to investigate the foundation for this, and I am hoping that I have laid the foundation with some degree of accuracy in attempting to set a background for the development of the archetypes of our Logos. Have I left out anything or made any errors, or could you make any comments on my attempt to lay the foundation for the construction that our Logos used for the archetypes?

RA: I am Ra. Your queries are thoughtful.

QUESTIONER: Are they accurate, or have I made mistakes?

RA: I am Ra. There are no mistakes.

QUESTIONER: Let me put it this way. Have I made missteps in my analysis of what has led to the construction of the archetypes that we experience?

RA: I am Ra. We may share with you the observation that judgment is no part of interaction between mind/body/spirit complexes. We have attempted to answer each query as fully as your language and the extent of your previous information allow. We may suggest that if, in perusing this present material, you have further queries, refining any concept, these queries may be asked and, again, we shall attempt adequate rejoinders.

QUESTIONER: I understand your limitations in answering that. Thank you.

Could you tell me how, in the first density, wind and fire teach earth and water?

RA: I am Ra. You may see the air and fire of that which is chaos as literally illuminating and forming the formless, for earth and water were, in the timeless state, unformed. As the active principles of fire and air blow and burn incandescently about that which nurtures that which is to come, the water learns to become sea, lake, and river, offering the opportunity for viable life. The earth learns to be shaped, thus offering the opportunity for viable life.

QUESTIONER: Are the seven archetypes for mind a function of or related to the seven densities that are to be experienced in the octave?

RA: I am Ra. The relationship is tangential in that no congruency may be seen. However, the progress through the archetypes has some of the characteristics of the progress through the densities. These relationships may be viewed without being, shall we say, pasted one upon the other.

QUESTIONER: How about the seven bodily energy centers? Are they related to archetypes in some way?

RA: I am Ra. The same may be said of these. It is informative to view the relationships but stifling to insist upon the limitations of congruency. Recall at all times, if you would use this term, that the archetypes are a portion of the resources of the mind complex.

QUESTIONER: Is there any relationship between the archetypes and the planets of our solar system?

RA: I am Ra. This is not a simple query. Properly, the archetypes have some relationship to the planets. However, this relationship is not one which can be expressed in your language. This, however, has not halted those among your people who have become adepts from attempting to name and describe these relationships. To most purely understand, if we may use this misnomer, the archetypes, it is well to view the concepts which make up each archetype and reserve the study of planets and other correspondences for meditation.

QUESTIONER: It just seemed to me that since the planets were an outgrowth of the Logos and since the archetypical mind was the foundation of the experience that the planets of this Logos would be somewhat related. We will certainly follow your suggestion.

I have been trying to get a foothold into an undistorted perception, you might say, of the archetypical mind. It seems to me that everything that I have read having to do with archetypes has been, to some degree or another, distorted by the writers and by the fact that our language is not really capable of description.

You have spoken of the Magician as a basic archetype, and that this seems to have been carried through from the previous octave. Would this be in order—if there is an order—the first archetypical concept for this Logos, the concept that we call the Magician?

RA: I am Ra. We would first respond to your confusion as regards the various writings upon the archetypical mind. You may well consider the very informative difference between a thing in itself and its relationships or functions. There is much study of archetype which is actually the study of functions, relationships, and correspondences. The study of planets, for instance, is an example of archetype seen as function. However, the archetypes are, first and most profoundly, things in themselves, and the pondering of them and their purest relationships with each other should be the most useful foundation for the study of the archetypical mind.

We now address your query as to the archetype which is the Matrix of the Mind. As to its name, the name of Magician is understandable when you consider that consciousness is the great foundation, mystery, and revelation which makes this particular density possible. The self-conscious entity is full of the magic of that which is to come. It may be considered first, for the mind is the first of the complexes to be developed by the student of spiritual evolution.

QUESTIONER: Would the archetype then that has been called the High Priestess, which represents the intuition, be properly the second of the archetypes?

RA: I am Ra. This is correct. You see here the recapitulation of the beginning knowledge of this Logos; that is, matrix and potentiator. The unconscious is indeed what may be poetically described as High Priestess, for it is the Potentiator of the Mind, and as potentiator for the mind is that principle which potentiates all experience.

QUESTIONER: Then for the third archetype, would the Empress be correct and be related to disciplined meditation?

RA: I am Ra. I perceive a mind complex intention of a query but was aware only of sound vibratory statement. Please requestion.

QUESTIONER. I was asking if the third archetype was the Empress, and was it correct to say that this archetype had to do with disciplined meditation?

RA: I am Ra. The third archetype may broadly be grasped as the Catalyst of the Mind. Thus it takes in far more than disciplined meditation. However, it is certainly through this faculty that catalyst is most efficiently used. The Archetype, Three, is perhaps confusedly called

Empress, although the intention of this number is the understanding that it represents the unconscious or female portion of the mind complex, being first, shall we say, used or ennobled by the male or conscious portion of the mind. Thus the noble name.

QUESTIONER: The fourth archetype is called The Emperor and seems to have to do with experience of other-selves and the green-ray energy center with respect to other-selves. Is this correct?

RA: I am Ra. This is perceptive. The broad name for Archetype Four may be the Experience of the Mind. In the Tarot you find the name of Emperor. Again this implies nobility, and in this case we may see the suggestion that it is only through the catalyst which has been processed by the potentiated consciousness that experience may ensue. Thusly is the conscious mind ennobled by the use of the vast resources of the unconscious mind.

This instrument's dorsal side grows stiff, and the instrument tires. We welcome one more query.

QUESTIONER: I would like to ask the reason for this session having been longer than most previous sessions, and also if there is anything that we can do to make the instrument more comfortable or to improve the contact?

RA: I am Ra. This instrument was given far more than the, shall we say, usual amount of transferred energy. There is a limit to the amount of energy of this type which may, with safety, be used when the instrument is, itself, without physical reserves. This is inevitable due to the various distortions such as we mentioned previously in this working having to do with growing dorsal discomfort.

The alignments are fastidious. We appreciate your conscientiousness. In order to enhance the comfort of the instrument, it might be suggested that careful manipulation of the dorsal area be accomplished before a working.

It is also suggested that, due to the attempt at psychic attack, this instrument will require warmth along the right side of the physical complex. There has been some infringement, but it should not be long lasting. It is, however, well to swaddle this instrument sufficiently to ward off any manifestation of this cold in physical form.

I am Ra. I leave you, my friends, in the love and in the light of the One Infinite Creator. Go forth, therefore, merrily rejoicing in the power and in the peace of the One Infinite Creator. Adonai.

Session 79,
February 24, 1982

RA: I am Ra. I greet you in the love and in the light of the One Infinite Creator. We communicate now.

QUESTIONER: Could you first give me the condition of the instrument?

RA: I am Ra. It is as previously stated.

QUESTIONER: The instrument would like to ask if there is any danger in the instrument receiving too much transferred energy in her present condition.

RA: I am Ra. No.

QUESTIONER: She would like to know the function of the energy transfer during the session.

RA: I am Ra. The function of this energy transfer is a most helpful one in that it serves to strengthen the shuttle through which the instreaming contact is received. The contact itself will monitor the condition of the instrument and cease communication when the distortions of the instrument begin to fluctuate towards the distortions of weakness or pain. However, while the contact is ongoing, the strength of the channel through which this contact flows may be aided by the energy transfer of which you spoke.

QUESTIONER: We have been ending our banishing ritual prior to the session by a gesture that relieves us of the magical personality. I was just wondering if we should maintain this personality and omit that gesture while we are walking the Circle of One and then relinquish the magical personality only after the circle is formed or after the session? Which would be more appropriate?

RA: I am Ra. The practice of magical workings demands the most rigorous honesty. If your estimate of your ability is that you can sustain the magical personality throughout this working, it is well. As long as you have some doubt, it is inadvisable. In any case it is appropriate for this instrument to return its magical personality rather than carry this persona into the trance state, for it does not have the requisite magical skill to function in this circumstance and would be far more vulnerable than if the waking personality is offered as channel. This working is indeed magical in nature in the basic sense. However, it is inappropriate to move more quickly than one's feet may walk.

QUESTIONER: I would like to question about the third-density experience of those entities just prior to the original extension of the first distortion to the sub-Logoi to create the split of polarity. Can you describe, in general, the differences between the third-density experience of these mind/body/spirits and the ones who have evolved upon this planet now?

RA: I am Ra. This material has been previously covered. Please query for specific interest.

QUESTIONER: Specifically, in the experience where only the service-to-others polarity in third density evolved, was the veil that was drawn with respect to knowledge of previous incarnations etc. in effect for those entities?

RA: I am Ra. No.

QUESTIONER: Was the reincarnational process like the one that we experience here, in which the third-density body is entered and exited numerous times during the cycle?

RA: I am Ra. This is correct.

QUESTIONER: Is it possible to give a time of incarnation with respect to our years, and would you do so if it is?

RA: I am Ra. The optimal incarnative period is somewhere close to a measure you call a millennium. This is, as you may say, a constant regardless of other factors of the third-density experience.

QUESTIONER: Then prior to the first extension of the first distortion, the veil or loss of awareness did not occur. From this I will make the assumption that this veil or loss of remembering consciously that which occurred before the incarnation was the primary tool for extending the first distortion. Is this correct?

RA: I am Ra. Your correctness is limited. This was the first tool.

QUESTIONER: Then from that statement I assume that the Logos first devised the tool of separating the unconscious from the conscious during what we call physical incarnations to achieve Its objective? Is this correct?

RA: I am Ra. Yes.

QUESTIONER: Then from that statement I would also assume that many other tools were conceived and used after the first tool of the so-called veil. Is this correct?

RA: I am Ra. There have been refinements.

QUESTIONER: The archetypical mind of the Logos prior to this experiment in veiling was what I would consider to be less complex than it is now, possibly containing fewer archetypes. Is this correct?

RA: I am Ra. We must ask your patience. We perceive a sudden flare of the distortion known as pain in this instrument's left arm and manual appendages. Please do not touch this instrument. We shall examine the mind complex and attempt to reposition the limb so that the working may continue. Then please repeat the query.

[Ninety-second pause]

I am Ra. You may proceed.

QUESTIONER: Thank you. Prior to the experiment to extend the first distortion, how many archetypes were there at that time?

RA: I am Ra. There were nine.

QUESTIONER: I will guess that those nine were three of mind, three of body, and three of spirit. Is this correct?

RA: I am Ra. This is correct.

QUESTIONER: I am going to guess that in the system of the Tarot, those archetypes would roughly correspond to, for the mind, The Magician, The Emperor, and The Chariot. Is this correct?

RA: I am Ra. This is incorrect.

QUESTIONER: Could you tell me what they correspond to?

RA: I am Ra. The body, the mind, and the spirit each contained and functioned under the aegis of the matrix, the potentiator, and the significator. The significator of the mind, body, and spirit is not identical to the significator of the mind, body, and spirit complexes.

QUESTIONER: I now understand what you meant in the previous session by saying that to extend free will, the significator must become a complex. It seems that the significator has become the complex that is the third, fourth, fifth, sixth, and seventh of the mind, the tenth on of the body, and the seventeenth on of the spirit. Is this correct?

RA: I am Ra. This is incorrect.

QUESTIONER: Could you tell me what you mean by "the significator must become a complex"?

RA: I am Ra. To be complex is to consist of more than one characteristic element or concept.

QUESTIONER: I would like to try to understand the archetypes of the mind of this Logos prior to the extension of the first distortion. In order to better understand that which we experience now, I believe that this is a logical approach.

We have, as you have stated, the matrix, the potentiator, and the significator. I understand the matrix as being that which is what we call the conscious mind, but since it is also that from which the mind is made, I am at a loss to fully understand these three terms, especially with respect to the time before there was a division in consciousness. Could you expand even more upon the Matrix of the Mind, the Potentiator of the Mind, and the Significator of the Mind, how they differ, and what their relationships are, please?

RA: I am Ra. The Matrix of Mind is that from which all comes. It is unmoving yet is the activator in potentiation of all mind activity. The Potentiator of the Mind is that great resource which may be seen as the sea into which the consciousness dips ever deeper and more thoroughly in order to create, ideate, and become more self-conscious.

The Significator of each mind, body, and spirit may be seen as a simple and unified concept. The Matrix of the Body may be seen to be a reflection in opposites of the mind; that is, unrestricted motion. The Potentiator of the Body then is that which, being informed, regulates activity.

The Matrix of the Spirit is difficult to characterize since the nature of spirit is less motile. The energies and movements of the spirit are, by far, the most profound yet, having more close association with time/space, do not have the characteristics of dynamic motion. Thusly one may see the Matrix as the deepest darkness and the Potentiator of Spirit as the most sudden awakening, illuminating, and generative influence.

This is the description of Archetypes One through Nine before the onset of influence of the co-Creator or sub-Logos's realization of free will.

QUESTIONER: The first change made then for this extension of free will was to make the communication between the Matrix and the Potentiator of the Mind relatively unavailable, one to the other, during the incarnation. Is this correct?

RA: I am Ra. We would perhaps rather term the condition as relatively more mystery filled than relatively unavailable.

QUESTIONER: The idea was then to create some type of veil between the Matrix and the Potentiator of the Mind. Is this correct?

RA: I am Ra. This is correct.

QUESTIONER: This veil then occurs between what we now call the unconscious and conscious minds. Is this correct?

RA: I am Ra. This is correct.

QUESTIONER: It was probably the design of the Logos to allow the conscious mind greater freedom under the first distortion by partitioning, you might say, this from the Potentiator or unconscious, which had a greater communication with the total mind, therefore, allowing for the birth of uneducated, to use a poor term, portions of consciousness. Is this correct?

RA: I am Ra. This is roughly correct.

QUESTIONER: Could you de-roughen it or elucidate a bit on that?

RA: I am Ra. There is intervening material before we may do so.

QUESTIONER: OK. Was then this simple experiment carried out and the product of this experiment observed before greater complexity was attempted?

RA: I am Ra. As we have said, there have been a great number of successive experiments.

QUESTIONER: I was just wondering since this seems to be the crux of the experiment, the large breaking point between no extension of the first distortion and the extension of the first distortion, what the result of this original experiment was with respect to that which was created from it. What was the result of that?

RA: I am Ra. This is previously covered material. The result of these experiments has been a more vivid, varied, and intense experience of Creator by Creator.

QUESTIONER: Well, I was aware of that. I probably didn't state the question correctly. It's a very difficult question to state. I don't know if it's worth attempting to continue with, but what I meant was when this very first experiment with the veiling process occurred, did it result in service-to-self polarization with the first experiment?

RA: I am Ra. The early, if we may use this term, Logoi produced service-to-self and service-to-others mind/body/spirit complexes immediately. The harvestability of these entities was not so immediate, and thus refinements of the archetypes began apace.

QUESTIONER: Now we are getting to what I was trying to determine. Then at this point, were there still only nine archetypes, and the veil had just been drawn between the Matrix and the Potentiator of the Mind?

RA: I am Ra. There were nine archetypes and many shadows.

QUESTIONER: By shadows do you mean the, what I might refer to as, birthing of small archetypical biases?

RA: I am Ra. Rather we would describe these shadows as the inchoate thoughts of helpful structures not yet fully conceived.

QUESTIONER: Would The Choice exist at this point during the creation of the first service-to-self polarity?

RA: I am Ra. Implicit in the veiling or separation of two archetypes is the concept of choice. The refinements to this concept took many experiences.

QUESTIONER: I'm sorry that I have so much difficulty in asking these questions, but this is material that I find somewhat difficult.

I find it interesting that the very first experiment of veiling the Matrix of the Mind from the Potentiator of the Mind and vice versa created service-to-self polarity. This seems to be a very important philosophical point in the development of the creation, and possibly the beginning of a system of what we would call magic not envisioned previously.

Let me ask this question. Prior to the extension of the first distortion, was the magical potential of the higher densities as great as it is now when the greatest potential was achieved in consciousness for each density? This is difficult to ask. What I am asking is that at the end of fourth density, prior to the extension of free will, was what we call magical potential as great as it is now at the end of fourth density?

RA: I am Ra. As you understand, if we may use this misnomer, magic, the magical potential in third and fourth density was then far greater than after the change. However, there was far, far less desire or will to use this potential.

QUESTIONER: Now, to be sure that I understand you: prior to the change and the extension of free will, let's take specifically the end of fourth density, magical potential for the condition when there was only service-to-others polarization was much greater at the end of fourth density than at the end of fourth density immediately after the split of polarization and the extension of free will. Is that correct?

RA: I am Ra. Magical ability is the ability to consciously use the so-called unconscious. Therefore, there was maximal ability prior to the innovation of sub-Logoi's free will.

QUESTIONER: OK. At the present time we are experiencing the effects of a more complex or greater number of archetypes, and I have guessed that the ones we are experiencing now in the mind are as follows: we have the Magician and High Priestess, which correspond to the Matrix and Potentiator with the veil drawn between them, which is the primary creator of the extension of the first distortion. Is that correct?

RA: I am Ra. We are unable to answer this query without intervening material.

QUESTIONER: OK. Sorry about that.

The next archetype, the Empress, is the Catalyst of the Mind, that which acts upon the conscious mind to change it. The fourth archetype is the Emperor, the Experience of the Mind, which is that material stored in the unconscious which creates its continuing bias. Am I correct with those statements?

RA: I am Ra. Though far too rigid in your statements, you perceive correct relationships. There is a great deal of dynamic interrelationship in these first four archetypes.

QUESTIONER: Would the Hierophant then be somewhat of a governor or sorter of these effects so as to create the proper assimilation by the unconscious of that which comes through the conscious?

RA: I am Ra. Although thoughtful, the supposition is incorrect in its heart.

QUESTIONER: What would be the Hierophant?

RA: I am Ra. The Hierophant is the Significator of the Body (Mind)[2] complex, its very nature. We may note that the characteristics of which you speak do have bearing upon the Significator of the Mind complex but are not the heart. The heart of the mind complex is that dynamic entity which absorbs, seeks, and attempts to learn.

QUESTIONER: Then is the Hierophant that link, you might say, between the mind and the body?

RA: I am Ra. There is a strong relationship between the significators of the mind, the body, and the spirit. Your statement is too broad.

QUESTIONER: Let me skip over the Hierophant for a minute, because I am really not understanding that at all and just ask if the Lovers represent a merging of the conscious and the unconscious or the communication of the conscious and unconscious?

RA: I am Ra. Again, without being at all unperceptive, you miss the heart of this particular archetype, which may be more properly called the Transformation of the Mind.

---

2. Ra corrected this error in Session 80. The Hierophant is the Significator of the Mind.

QUESTIONER: Transformation of the mind into what?

RA: I am Ra. As you observe Archetype Six, you may see the student of the mysteries being transformed by the need to choose betwixt the light and the dark in mind.

QUESTIONER: Would the Conqueror or Chariot then represent the culmination of the action of the first six archetypes into a conquering of the mental processes, even possibly removing the veil?

RA: I am Ra. This is most perceptive. The Archetype Seven is one difficult to enunciate. We may call it the Path, the Way, or the Great Way of the Mind. Its foundation is a reflection and substantial summary of Archetypes One through Six.

One may also see the Way of the Mind as showing the kingdom or fruits of appropriate travel through the mind, in that the mind continues to move as majestically through the material it conceives of as a chariot drawn by royal lions or steeds.

At this time we would suggest one more full query, for this instrument is experiencing some distortions towards pain.

QUESTIONER: Then I will just ask about the one of the archetypes which I am the least able to understand at this point, if I can use that word at all. I am still very much in the dark, so to speak, in respect to the Hierophant and precisely what it is. Could you give me some other indication of what that is?

RA: I am Ra. You have been most interested in the Significator, which must needs become complex. The Hierophant is the original archetype of mind, which has been made complex through the subtle movements of the conscious and unconscious. The complexities of mind were evolved rather than the simple melding of experience from Potentiator to Matrix.

The mind itself became an actor possessed of free will and, more especially, will. As the Significator of the mind, The Hierophant has the will to know, but what shall it do with its knowledge, and for what reasons does it seek? The potentials of a complex significator are manifold.

Are there any brief queries at this working?

QUESTIONER: Only is there anything that we can do to make the instrument more comfortable or to improve the contact?

RA: I am Ra. All is well. For some small portion of your future, the instrument would be well advised to wear upon the hands those aids to comfort which it has neglected to use. There has been some trauma to both hands and arms, and, therefore, we have had to somewhat abbreviate this working.

I am Ra. You are conscientious, my friends. We leave you in the love and in the light of the One Infinite Creator. Go forth, therefore, rejoicing in the power and the peace of the One Glorious Infinite Creator. Adonai.

Session 80,
February 27, 1982

RA: I am Ra. We greet you in the love and in the light of the One Infinite Creator.

Before we initiate this working, we would wish to correct an error which we have found in previous material. That Archetype Five, which you have called the Hierophant, is the Significator of the Mind complex.

This instrument is prey to sudden flares towards the distortion known as pain. We are aware of your conscientious attempts to aid the instrument, but know of no other modality available to the support group other than the provision of water therapy upon the erect spinal portion of the physical-body complex, which we have previously mentioned.

This instrument's distortions of body do not ever rule out, shall we say, such flares during these periods of increased distortion of the body complex. Our contact may become momentarily garbled. Therefore, we request that any information which seems garbled be questioned, as we wish this contact to remain as undistorted as the limitations of language, mentality, and sensibility allow.

We communicate now.

QUESTIONER: Thank you. Could you please give me the condition of the instrument?

RA: I am Ra. This instrument is experiencing mild fluctuations of the physical-energy complex, which are causing sudden changes from physical energy deficit to some slight physical energy. This is due to many, what you may call, prayers and affirmations offered to and by the instrument, offset by continual greetings whenever it is feasible by the fifth-density entity of whom you are aware.

In other respects, the instrument is in the previously stated condition.

QUESTIONER: I had to leave the room for a forgotten item after we performed the banishing ritual. Did this have a deleterious effect on the ritual or the working?

RA: I am Ra. Were it the only working, the lapse would have been critical. There is enough residual energy of a protective nature in this place of working that this lapse, though quite unrecommended, does not represent a threat to the protection which the ritual of which you spoke offers.

QUESTIONER: Has our fifth-density visitor been less able to affect the instrument during our more recent workings?

RA: I am Ra. We shall answer in two parts. Firstly, during the workings themselves the entity has been bated to a great extent. Secondly, in the general experiential circumstances of your space/time experience, this fifth-density entity is able to greet this entity with the same effectiveness upon the physical-body complex as always since the inception of its contact with your group. This is due to the several physical-complex distortions of the instrument.

However, the instrument has become more mentally and spiritually able to greet this entity with love, thereby reducing the element of fear, which is an element the entity counts as a great weapon in the attempt to cause cessation, in any degree, of the Ra contact.

QUESTIONER: What is the reason for the fact that the entity is able to act through physical distortions that are already present, as opposed to being unable to act upon an entity who has no physical distortion at all?

RA: I am Ra. The key to this query is the term "distortion." Any distortion, be it physical, mental, or spiritual in complex nature, may be accentuated by the suggestion of one able to work magically; that is, to cause changes in consciousness. This entity has many physical distortions. Each in the group has various mental distortions. Their nature varies. The less balanced the distortion by self-knowledge, the more adeptly the entity may accentuate such a distortion in order to mitigate against the smooth functioning and harmony of the group.

QUESTIONER: As Ra well knows, the information that we accumulate here will be illuminating to a very minor percentage of those who populate this planet, simply because there are very few people who can understand it. However, it seems that our fifth-density visitor is, shall we say, dead set against this communication. Can you tell me why this is so important to him, since it is of such a limited effect, I would guess, upon the harvest of this planet?

RA: I am Ra. Purity does not end with the harvest of third density. The fidelity of Ra towards the attempt to remove distortions is total. This constitutes an acceptance of responsibility for service to others, which is of relative purity. The instrument through which we speak and its support group have a similar fidelity and, disregarding any inconvenience to self, desire to serve others. Due to the nature of the group, the queries made to us by the group have led rapidly into somewhat abstruse regions of commentary. This content does not mitigate against the underlying purity of the contact. Such purity is as a light. Such an intensity of light attracts attention.

QUESTIONER: What would our fifth-density visitor hope to gain for himself if he were to be successful in eliminating this contact?

RA: I am Ra. As we have previously stated, the entity hopes to gain a portion of that light; that is, the mind/body/spirit complex of the instrument. Barring this, the entity intends to put out the light.

QUESTIONER: I understand this up to a point, and that point is if the entity were successful in either of these attempts, of what value would this be to him? Would it increase his ability? Would it increase his polarity? By what mechanism would it do whatever it does?

RA: I am Ra. Having attempted for some of your space/time, with no long-lasting result, to do these things, the entity may be asking this question of itself. The gain for triumph is an increase in negative polarity to the entity, in that it has removed a source of radiance and, thereby, offered to this space/time the opportunity of darkness where there once was light. In the event that it succeeded in enslaving the mind/body/spirit complex of the instrument, it would have enslaved a fairly powerful entity, thus adding to its power.

QUESTIONER: I am sorry for my lack of penetration of these mechanisms, and I apologize for some rather stupid questions, but I think we have here a point that is somewhat central to what we are presently attempting to understand. Some of my next questions may be almost unacceptably stupid, but I will attempt to try to understand what this power that our visitor seeks is and how he uses it. It seems to me that this is central to the mind and its evolution.

As our visitor increases his power through these works, what is the power that he increases? Can you describe it?

RA: I am Ra. The power of which you speak is a spiritual power. The powers of the mind, as such, do not encompass such works as these. You may, with some fruitfulness, consider the possibilities of moonlight. You are aware that we have described the Matrix of the Spirit as a Night. The moonlight, then, offers either a true picture seen in shadow or chimera and falsity. The power of falsity is deep, as is the power to discern truth from shadow. The shadow of hidden things is an infinite depth in which is stored the power of the One Infinite Creator.

The adept, then, is working with the power of hidden things illuminated by that which can be false or true. To embrace falsity, to know it, and to seek it, and to use it, gives a power that is most great. This is the nature of the power of your visitor and may shed some light upon the power of one who seeks in order to serve others as well, for the missteps in the night are oh! so easy.

QUESTIONER: Are you saying, then, that this power is of the spirit and not of the mind or of the body?

RA: I am Ra. The work of the adept is based upon previous work with the mind and the body; else, work with the spirit would not be possible on a dependable basis. With this comment we may assert the correctness of your assumption.

QUESTIONER: The fifteenth archetype is the Matrix of the Spirit and has been called the Devil. Can you tell me why that is so?

RA: I am Ra. We do not wish to be facile in such a central query, but we may note that the nature of the spirit is so infinitely subtle that the fructifying influence of light upon the great darkness of the spirit is very often not as apparent as the darkness itself. The progress chosen by many adepts becomes a confused path as each adept attempts to use the Catalyst of the Spirit. Few there are which are successful in grasping the light of the sun. By far, the majority of adepts remain groping in the moonlight, and, as we have said, this light can deceive as well as uncover hidden mystery. Therefore, the melody, shall we say, of this matrix often seems to be of a negative and evil, as you would call it, nature.

It is also to be noted that an adept is one which has freed itself more and more from the constraints of the thoughts, opinions, and bonds of other-selves. Whether this is done for service to others or service to self, it is a necessary part of the awakening of the adept. This freedom is seen by those not free as what you would call evil or black. The magic is recognized; the nature is often not.

QUESTIONER: Could I say, then, that implicit in the process of becoming adept is the seeming polarization towards service-to-self, because the adept becomes disassociated with many of his kind?

RA: I am Ra. This is likely to occur. The apparent happening is disassociation, whether the truth is service to self and thus true disassociation from other-selves or service to others, and thus true association with the heart of all other-selves and disassociation only from the illusory husks which prevent the adept from correctly perceiving the self and other-self as one.

QUESTIONER: Then you say that this effect of disassociation on the service-to-others adept is a stumbling block or slowing process in reaching that goal to which he aspires? Is this correct?

RA: I am Ra. This is incorrect. This disassociation from the miasma of illusion and misrepresentation of each and every distortion is a quite necessary portion of an adept's path. It may be seen by others to be unfortunate.

QUESTIONER: Then is this, from the point of view of the fifteenth archetype, somewhat of an excursion into the Matrix of the Spirit in this process? Does that make any sense?

RA: I am Ra. The excursion of which you speak and the process of disassociation is most usually linked with that archetype you call Hope, which we would prefer to call Faith. This archetype is the Catalyst of the Spirit and, because of the illuminations of the Potentiator of the Spirit, will begin to cause these changes in the adept's viewpoint.

QUESTIONER: I didn't intend to get too far ahead of my questioning process here. The positively or negatively polarized adept, then, is building a potential to draw directly on the spirit for power. Is this correct?

RA: I am Ra. It would be more proper to say that the adept is calling directly through the spirit to the universe for its power, for the spirit is a shuttle.

QUESTIONER: The only obvious significant difference, I believe, between the positive and negative adepts in using this shuttle is the way they polarize. Is there a relationship between the archetypes of the spirit and whether the polarization is either positive or negative? Is, for instance, the positive calling through the sixteenth archetype and the negative calling through the fifteenth archetype? I am very confused about this, and I imagine that that question is either poor or meaningless. Can you answer that?

RA: I am Ra. It is a challenge to answer such a query, for there is some confusion in its construction. However, we shall attempt to speak upon the subject.

The adept, whether positive or negative, has the same Matrix. The Potentiator is also identical. Due to the Catalyst of each adept, the adept may begin to pick and choose that into which it shall look further. The Experience of the Spirit, that which you have called the Moon, is then, by far, the more manifest of influences upon the polarity of the adept. Even the most unhappy of experiences, shall we say, which seem to occur in the Catalyst of the adept, seen from the viewpoint of the spirit, may, with the discrimination possible in shadow, be worked with until light equaling the light of brightest noon descends upon the adept, and positive or service-to-others illumination has occurred. The service-to-self adept will satisfy itself with the shadows and, grasping the light of day, will toss back the head in grim laughter, preferring the darkness.

QUESTIONER: I guess the nineteenth archetype of the spirit would be the Significator of the Spirit. Is that correct?

RA: I am Ra. This is correct.

QUESTIONER: How would you describe the Significator of the Spirit?

RA: I am Ra. In answer to the previous query, we set about doing just this. The Significator of the Spirit is that living entity which either radiates or absorbs the love and the light of the One Infinite Creator, radiates it to others or absorbs it for the self.

QUESTIONER: Then would this process of radiation or absorption, since we have what I would call a flux or flux rate, be the measure of the adept?

RA: I am Ra. This may be seen to be a reasonably adequate statement.

QUESTIONER: Then for the twentieth archetype, I'm guessing that this is the Transformation of the Spirit, possibly analogous to the sixth-density merging of the paths. Is this in any way correct?

RA: I am Ra. No.

QUESTIONER: Sorry about that. Can you tell me what the twentieth archetype would be?

RA: I am Ra. That which you call the Sarcophagus in your system may be seen to be the material world, if you will. This material world is transformed by the spirit into that which is infinite and eternal. The infinity of the spirit is an even-greater realization than the infinity of consciousness, for consciousness which has been disciplined by will and faith is that consciousness which may contact intelligent infinity directly. There are many things which fall away in the many, many steps of adepthood. We, of Ra, still walk these steps and praise the One Infinite Creator at each transformation.

QUESTIONER: Then I would guess that the twenty-first archetype would represent contact with intelligent infinity. Is that correct?

RA: I am Ra. This is correct, although one may also see the reflection of this contact as well as the contact with intelligent energy which is the Universe or, as you have called it somewhat provincially, the World.

QUESTIONER: Then by this contact also with intelligent energy, can you give me an example of what this would be for both the contact with intelligent infinity and the contact with intelligent energy? Could you give me an example of what type of experience this would result in, if that is at all possible?

RA: I am Ra. This shall be the last query of this working of full length. We have discussed the possibilities of contact with intelligent energy, for this energy is the energy of the Logos, and thus it is the energy which heals, builds, removes, destroys, and transforms all other-selves as well as the self.

The contact with intelligent infinity is most likely to produce an unspeakable joy in the entity experiencing such contact. If you wish to query in more detail upon this subject, we invite you to do so in another working. Is there a brief query before we close this working?

QUESTIONER: Is there anything that we can do to improve the contact or to make the instrument more comfortable?

RA: I am Ra. The alignments are most conscientious. We are appreciative. The entity which serves as instrument is somewhat distorted towards that condition you call stiffness of the dorsal regions. Manipulation would be helpful.

I am Ra. I leave you, my friends, glorying in the light and the love of the One Infinite Creator. Go forth, therefore, rejoicing in the power and in the peace of the One Infinite Creator. Adonai.

Session 81,
March 22, 1982

RA: I am Ra. I greet you in the love and in the light of the One Infinite Creator. We communicate now.

QUESTIONER: Could you first tell me the condition of the instrument?

RA: I am Ra. The physical-complex energy is in deficit at this particular space/time nexus due to prolonged psychic accentuation of preexisting distortions. The remainder of the energy complex levels are as previously stated.

QUESTIONER: Is this the reason for the instrument's feeling of uninterrupted weariness?

RA: I am Ra. There are portions of your space/time in which this may be said to be symptomatic of the psychic-greeting reaction. However, the continual weariness is not due to psychic greeting but is rather an inevitable consequence of this contact.

QUESTIONER: Why is this an inevitable consequence? What is the mechanism of this contact that creates this weariness?

RA: I am Ra. The mechanism creating weariness is that connection betwixt the density wherein this instrument's mind/body/spirit complex is safely kept during these workings, and the altogether variant density in which the instrument's physical-body complex resides at this space/time. As the instrument takes on more of the coloration of the resting density, the third-density experience seems more heavy and wearisome. This was accepted by the instrument, as it desired to be of service. Therefore, we accept also this effect, about which nothing of which we are aware may be done.

QUESTIONER: Is the effect a function of the number of sessions, and has it reached a peak level or will it continue to increase in effect?

RA: I am Ra. This wearying effect will continue but should not be confused with the physical energy levels, having only to do with the, as you would call it, daily round of experience. In this sphere, those things which are known already to aid this instrument will continue to be of aid. You will, however, notice the gradual increase in transparency, shall we say, of the vibrations of the instrument.

QUESTIONER: I didn't understand what you meant by that last statement. Could you explain it?

RA: I am Ra. Weariness of the time/space nature may be seen to be that reaction of transparent or pure vibrations with impure, confused, or opaque environs.

QUESTIONER: Is there any of this effect upon the other two of us in this group?

RA: I am Ra. This is quite correct.

QUESTIONER: Then we would also experience the uninterrupted weariness as a consequence of the contact. Is this correct?

RA: I am Ra. The instrument, by the very nature of the contact, bears the brunt of this effect. Each of the support group, by offering the love and the light of the One Infinite Creator in unqualified support in these workings and in energy transfers for the purpose of these workings, experiences between 10 and 15 percent, roughly, of this effect. It is cumulative and identical in the continual nature of its manifestation.

QUESTIONER: What could be the result of this continued wearying effect after a long period?

RA: I am Ra. You ask a general query with infinite answers. We shall overgeneralize in order to attempt to reply.

One group might be tempted and thus lose the very contact which caused the difficulty. So the story would end.

Another group might be strong at first but not faithful in the face of difficulty. Thus the story would end.

Another group might choose the path of martyrdom in its completeness and use the instrument until its physical-body complex failed from the harsh toll demanded when all energy was gone.

This particular group, at this particular nexus, is attempting to conserve the vital energy of the instrument. It is attempting to balance love of service and wisdom of service, and it is faithful to the service in the face of difficulty. Temptation has not yet ended this group's story.

We may not know the future, but the probability of this situation continuing over a relatively substantial period of your space/time is large. The significant factor is the will of the instrument and of the group to serve. That is the only cause for balancing the slowly increasing weariness, which will continue to distort your perceptions. Without this will, the contact might be possible but finally seem too much of an effort.

QUESTIONER: The instrument would like to know why she has a feeling of increased vital energy.

RA: I am Ra. We leave this answer to the instrument.

QUESTIONER: She would like to know if she has an increased sensitivity to foods.

RA: I am Ra. This instrument has an increased sensitivity to all stimuli. It is well that it use prudence.

QUESTIONER: Going back to the previous session, picking up on the tenth archetype, which is the Catalyst of the Body, the Wheel of Fortune represents interaction with other-selves. Is this a correct statement?

RA: I am Ra. This may be seen to be a roughly correct statement in that each catalyst is dealing with the nature of those experiences entering the energy web and vibratory perceptions of the mind/body/

spirit complex. The most carefully noted addition would be that the outside stimulus of the Wheel of Fortune is that which offers both positive and negative experience.

QUESTIONER: The eleventh archetype would then be the Experience of the Body, which represents the catalyst which has been processed by the mind/body/spirit complex and is called the Enchantress because it produces further seed for growth. Is this correct?

RA: I am Ra. This is correct.

QUESTIONER: We have already discussed the Significator, so I will skip number thirteen. The Transformation of the Body is called Death, for with death the body is transformed to a higher vibrational body for additional learning. Is this correct?

RA: I am Ra. This is correct and may be seen to be additionally correct in that each moment and certainly each diurnal period of the bodily incarnation offers death and rebirth to one which is attempting to use the catalyst which is offered it.

QUESTIONER: Finally, the fourteenth, the Way of the Body, is called the Alchemist because there is an infinity of time for the various bodies to operate within to learn the lessons necessary for evolution. Is this correct?

RA: I am Ra. This is less than completely correct, as the Great Way of the Body must be seen, as are all the archetypes of the body, to be a mirror image of the thrust of the activity of the mind. The body is the creature of the mind and is the instrument of manifestation for the fruits of mind and spirit. Therefore, you may see the body as providing the athanor[3] through which the Alchemist manifests gold.

QUESTIONER: I have guessed that the way to enter into a better comprehension of the archetypes is to compare what we experience now, after the veil, with what was experienced prior to that time, starting possibly as far back as the beginning of this octave of experience, to see how we got into the condition that we are in now. If this is agreeable, I would like to retreat to the very beginning of this octave of experience to investigate the conditions of mind, body, and spirit as they evolved in this octave. Is this acceptable?

---

3. athanor: an oven; a fire; a digesting furnace, formerly used in alchemy, so constructed as to maintain a uniform and constant heat.

RA: I am Ra. The direction of questions is your provenance.

QUESTIONER: Ra states that it has knowledge of only this octave, but it seems that Ra has complete knowledge of this octave. Can you tell me why this is?

RA: I am Ra. Firstly, we do not have complete knowledge of this octave. There are portions of the seventh density which, although described to us by our teachers, remain mysterious. Secondly, we have experienced a great deal of the available refining catalyst of this octave, and our teachers have worked with us most carefully that we may be one with all, that in turn our eventual returning to the great allness of creation shall be complete.

QUESTIONER: Then Ra has knowledge from the first beginnings of this octave through its present experience and what I might call direct or experiential knowledge through communication with those space/times and time/spaces, but has not yet evolved to or penetrated the seventh level. Is this a roughly correct statement?

RA: I am Ra. Yes.

QUESTIONER: Why does Ra not have any knowledge of that which was prior to the beginning of this octave?

RA: I am Ra. Let us compare octaves to islands. It may be that the inhabitants of an island are not alone upon a planetary sphere, but if an ocean-going vehicle in which one may survive has not been invented, true knowledge of other islands is possible only if an entity comes among the islanders and says, "I am from elsewhere." This is a rough analogy. However, we have evidence of this sort, both of previous creation and creation to be, as we in the stream of space/time and time/space view these apparently non-simultaneous events.

QUESTIONER: We presently find ourselves in the Milky Way galaxy of some 200 or so billion stars, and there are millions and millions of these large galaxies spread out through what we call space. To Ra's knowledge, can I assume that the number of these galaxies is infinite? Is this correct?

RA: I am Ra. This is precisely correct and is a significant point.

QUESTIONER: The point being that we have unity. Is that correct?

RA: I am Ra. You are perceptive.

QUESTIONER: Then what portion of these galaxies is Ra aware of? Has Ra experienced consciousness in many other of these galaxies?

RA: I am Ra. No.

QUESTIONER: Has Ra experienced or does Ra have any knowledge of any of these other galaxies? Has Ra traveled to, in one form or another, any of these other galaxies?

RA: I am Ra. Yes.

QUESTIONER: It's unimportant, but how many other of these galaxies has Ra traveled to?

RA: I am Ra. We have opened our hearts in radiation of love to the entire creation. Approximately 90 percent of the creation is at some level aware of the sending and able to reply. All of the infinite Logoi are one in the consciousness of love. This is the type of contact which we enjoy rather than travel.

QUESTIONER: So that I can just get a little idea of what I am talking about, what are the limits of Ra's travel in the sense of directly experiencing or seeing the activities of various places? Is it solely within this galaxy, and if so, how much of this galaxy? Or does it include some other galaxies?

RA: I am Ra. Although it would be possible for us to move at will throughout the creation within this Logos, that is to say, the Milky Way galaxy, so called, we have moved where we were called to service; these locations being, shall we say, local and including Alpha Centauri, planets of your solar system which you call the Sun, Cepheus, and Zeta Reticuli. To these sub-Logoi we have come, having been called.

QUESTIONER: Was the call in each instance from the third-density beings or was this call from other densities?

RA: I am Ra. In general, the latter supposition is correct. In the particular case of the Sun sub-Logos, third density is the density of calling.

QUESTIONER: Ra then has not moved at any time into one of the other major galaxies. Is this correct?

RA: I am Ra. This is correct.

QUESTIONER: Does Ra have knowledge of any other major galaxy or the consciousness of anything in that galaxy?

RA: I am Ra. We assume you are speaking of the possibility of knowledge of other major galaxies. There are Wanderers from other major galaxies drawn to the specific needs of a single call. There are those among our social memory complex which have become Wanderers in other major galaxies. Thus there has been knowledge of other major galaxies, for to one whose personality or mind/body/spirit complex has been crystallized, the universe is one place and there is no bar upon travel. However, our interpretation of your query was a query concerning the social memory complex traveling to another major galaxy. We have not done this, nor do we contemplate it, for we can reach in love with our hearts.

QUESTIONER: Thank you. In this line of questioning I am trying to establish a basis for understanding the foundation for not only the experience that we have now but how the experience was formed and how it is related to all the rest of the experience through the portion of the octave as we understand it. I am assuming, then, that all of these galaxies, this infinite number of galaxies that we can just begin to become aware of with our telescopes, are all of the same octave. Is this correct?

RA: I am Ra. This is correct.

QUESTIONER: I was wondering if some of the Wanderers from Ra in going to some of the other major galaxies—that is, leaving this system of some 200 billion stars of lenticular shape and going to another cluster of billions of stars and finding their way into some planetary situation there—would encounter the dual polarity that we have here, the service-to-self and the service-to-others polarities?

RA: I am Ra. This is correct.

QUESTIONER: You stated earlier that toward the center of this galaxy is what, to use a poor term, you could call the older portion where you would find no service-to-self polarization. Am I correct in assuming that this is true with the other galaxies with which Wanderers from Ra have experience? At the center of these galaxies, only the service-to-others polarity exists and the experiment started farther out toward the rim of the galaxy?

RA: I am Ra. Various Logoi and sub-Logoi had various methods of arriving at the discovery of the efficiency of free will in intensifying the experience of the Creator by the Creator. However, in each case this has been a pattern.

QUESTIONER: You mean then that the pattern is that the service-to-self polarization appeared farther out from the center of the galactic spiral?

RA: I am Ra. This is correct.

QUESTIONER: From this I will assume that from the beginning of the octave, we had the core of many galactic spirals forming, and I know that this is incorrect in the sense of timelessness, but as the spiral formed, then I am assuming that in this particular octave the experiment of the veiling and the extending of free will must have started, roughly, simultaneously in many, many of the budding or building galactic systems. Am I in any way correct with this assumption?

RA: I am Ra. You are precisely correct. This instrument is unusually fragile at this space/time and has used much of the transferred energy. We would invite one more full query for this working.

QUESTIONER: Actually, I don't have much more on this except to make the assumption that there must have been some type of communication throughout the octave so that, when the first experiment became effective, knowledge of this spread rapidly through the octave and was picked up by other budding galactic spirals, you might say. Is this correct?

RA: I am Ra. This is correct. To be aware of the nature of this communication is to be aware of the nature of the Logos. Much of what you call creation has never separated from the One Logos of this octave and resides within the One Infinite Creator. Communication in such an environment is the communication of cells of the body. That which is learned by one is known to all. The sub-Logoi, then, have been in the position of refining the discoveries of what might be called the earlier sub-Logoi. May we ask if we may answer any brief queries at this working?

QUESTIONER: Only if there is anything that we can do to make the instrument more comfortable or to improve the contact?

RA: I am Ra. It is difficult to determine the energy levels of the instrument and support group. Of this we are aware. It is, however, recommended that every attempt be made to enter each working with the most-desirable configurations of energy possible. All is well, my friends. You are conscientious and the alignments are well.

I am Ra. I leave you in the love and the light of the One Infinite Creator. Go forth, therefore, rejoicing in the power and in the peace of the Infinite Creator. Adonai.

Session 82,
March 27, 1982

RA: I am Ra. I greet you, my friends, in the love and in the light of the One Infinite Creator. We communicate now.

QUESTIONER: Could you first please give me the condition of the instrument?

RA: I am Ra. It is as previously stated.

QUESTIONER: Is there anything at all that we could do that we are not doing—besides eliminating the contact—to increase the physical energy of the instrument?

RA: I am Ra. There is the possibility/probability that the whirling of the water with spine erect would alter, somewhat, the distortion towards what you call pain which this entity experiences in the dorsal region on a continuous level. This in turn could aid in the distortion towards increase of physical energy to some extent.

QUESTIONER: I would like to consider the condition at a time or position just prior to the beginning of this octave of experience. I am assuming that, just prior to the beginning of this octave, intelligent infinity had created and already experienced one or more previous octaves. Is this correct?

RA: I am Ra. You assume correctly. However, the phrase would more informatively read infinite intelligence had experienced previous octaves.

QUESTIONER: Does Ra have any knowledge of the number of previous octaves; if so, how many?

RA: I am Ra. As far as we are aware, we are in an infinite creation. There is no counting.

QUESTIONER: That's what I thought you might say. Am I correct in assuming that at the beginning of this octave, out of what I would call a void of space, seeds of an infinite number of galactic systems such as the Milky Way galaxy appeared and grew in spiral fashion simultaneously?

RA: I am Ra. There are duple areas of potential confusion. Firstly, let us say that the basic concept is reasonably well stated. Now we address the confusions. The nature of true simultaneity is such that, indeed, all is simultaneous. However, in your modes of perception you would perhaps more properly view the seeding of the creation as that of growth from the center or core outward. The second confusion lies in the term "void." We would substitute the noun "plenum."

QUESTIONER: Then, if I were observing the beginning of the octave at that time through a telescope, say from this position, would I see the center of many, many galaxies appearing and each of them then spreading outward in a spiraling fashion over what we would consider billions of years, but the spirals spreading outward in approximately what we would consider the same rate so that all these galaxies began as the first speck of light at the same time and then spread out at roughly the same rate? Is this correct?

RA: I am Ra. The query has confusing elements. There is a center to infinity. From this center, all spreads. Therefore, there are centers to the creation, to the galaxies, to star systems, to planetary systems, and to consciousness. In each case you may see growth from the center outward. Thus you may see your query as being over-general in concept.

QUESTIONER: Considering only our Milky Way galaxy at its beginnings, I will assume that the first occurrence that we could find with our physical apparatus was the appearance of a star of the nature of our sun. Is this correct?

RA: I am Ra. In the case of the galactic systems, the first manifestation of the Logos is a cluster of central systems which generate the outward swirling energies producing, in their turn, further energy centers for the Logos or what you would call stars.

QUESTIONER: Are these central original creations or clusters what we call stars?

RA: I am Ra. This is correct. However, the closer to the, shall we say, beginning of the manifestation of the Logos the star is, the more it partakes in the one original thought.

QUESTIONER: Why does this partaking in the original thought have a gradient radially outward? That's the way I understand your statement.

RA: I am Ra. This is the plan of the One Infinite Creator. The One Original Thought is the harvest of all previous, if you would use this term, experience of the Creator by the Creator. As It decides to know Itself, It generates Itself, into that plenum full of the glory and the power of the One Infinite Creator which is manifested to your perceptions as space or outer space. Each generation of this knowing begets a knowing which has the capacity, through free will, to choose methods of knowing Itself. Therefore, gradually, step by step, the Creator becomes that which may know Itself, and the portions of the Creator partake less purely in the power of the original word or thought. The Creator does not properly create as much as It experiences Itself.

QUESTIONER: What was the form, condition, or experience of the first division of consciousness that occurred at the beginning of this octave at the beginning of this galactic experience?

RA: I am Ra. We touch upon previous material. The harvest of the previous octave was the Creator of Love manifested in mind, body, and spirit. This form of the Creator experiencing Itself may perhaps be said to be the first division.

QUESTIONER: I was interested specifically in how this very first division showed up in this octave. I was interested to know if it made the transition through first, second, third, fourth, etc. densities? I would like to take the first mind/body/spirit complexes and trace their experience from the very start to the present so that I could better understand the condition that we are in now by comparing it with this original growth. Could you please tell me precisely how this came about as to the formation of the planets and growth through the densities, if that is the way it happened, please?

RA: I am Ra. Your queries seem more confused than your basic mental distortions in this area. Let us speak in general and perhaps you may find a less confused and more simple method of eliciting information in this area.

A very great deal of creation was manifested without the use of the concepts involved in consciousness, as you know it. The creation itself is a form of consciousness which is unified, the Logos being the one great heart of creation. The process of evolution through this period, which may be seen to be timeless, is most valuable to take into consideration, for it is against the background of this essential unity of the fabric of creation that we find the ultimate development of the Logoi which chose to use that portion of the harvested consciousness of the Creator to move forward with the process of knowledge of self. As it had been found to be efficient to use the various densities, which are fixed in each octave, in order to create conditions in which self-conscious sub-Logoi could exist, this was carried out throughout the growing flower-strewn field, as your simile suggests, of the one infinite creation.

The first beings of mind, body, and spirit were not complex. The experience of mind/body/spirits at the beginning of this octave of experience was singular. There was no third-density forgetting. There was no veil. The lessons of third density are predestined by the very nature of the vibratory rates experienced during this particular density and by the nature of the quantum jump to the vibratory experiences of fourth density.

QUESTIONER: Am I correct, then, in assuming the first mind/body/ spirit experiences, as this galaxy progressed in growth, were those that moved through the densities; that is, the process we have discussed coming out of second density. For instance, let us take a particular planet, one of the very early planets formed near the center of the galaxy. I will assume that the planet solidified during the first density, that life appeared in second density, and that all of the mind/ body/spirit complexes of third density progressed out of second density on that planet and evolved in third density. Is this correct?

RA: I am Ra. This is hypothetically correct.

QUESTIONER: Did this in fact happen on some of the planets or on a large percentage of the planets near the center of this galaxy in this way?

RA: I am Ra. Our knowledge is limited. We know of the beginning but cannot asseverate to the precise experiences of those things occurring before us. You know the nature of historical teaching. At our level of learn/teaching we may expect little distortion. However, we cannot, with surety, say there is no distortion as we speak of specific occurrences of which we were not consciously a part. It is our understanding that your supposition is correct. Thus we so hypothesize.

QUESTIONER: Specifically, I am trying to grasp an understanding of the process of experience in third density before the veil so that I can better understand the present process. As I understand it, the mind/body/spirits went through the process of what we call physical incarnation in this density, but there was no forgetting. What was the benefit or purpose of the physical incarnation when there was no forgetting?

RA: I am Ra. The purpose of incarnation in third density is to learn the ways of love.

QUESTIONER: I guess I didn't state that exactly right. What I mean is, since there was no forgetting, since the mind/body/spirits had, in what we call the physical incarnation, their full consciousness, they knew the same thing that they would know while not in the physical incarnation. What was the mechanism of teaching that taught the ways of love in the third-density physical prior to the forgetting process?

RA: I am Ra. We ask your permission to answer this query in an oblique fashion, as we perceive an area in which we might be of aid.

QUESTIONER: Certainly.

RA: I am Ra. Your queries seem to be pursuing the possibility/probability that the mechanisms of experience in third density are different if a mind/body/spirit is attempting them rather than a mind/body/spirit complex. The nature of third density is constant. Its ways are to be learned the same now and ever. Thusly, no matter what form the entity facing these lessons, the lessons and mechanisms are the same. The Creator will learn from Itself. Each entity has unmanifest portions of learning and, most importantly, learning which is involved with other-selves.

QUESTIONER: Then prior to the forgetting process, there was no concept of anything but service-to-others polarization. What sort of societies and experiences in third density were created and evolved in this condition?

RA: I am Ra. It is our perception that such conditions created the situation of a most pallid experiential nexus in which lessons were garnered with the relative speed of the turtle to the cheetah.

QUESTIONER: Did such societies evolve with technologies of a complex nature, or did they remain quite simple? Can you give me a general idea of the evolvement that would be a function of what we would call intellectual activity?

RA: I am Ra. There is infinite diversity in societies under any circumstances. There were many highly technologically advanced societies which grew due to the ease of producing any desired result. When one dwells within what might be seen to be a state of constant potential inspiration, that which even the most highly sophisticated, in your terms, societal structure lacked, given the noncomplex nature of its entities, was what you might call will or, to use a more plebeian term, gusto, or élan vital.

QUESTIONER: Did such technological societies evolve travel through what we call space to other planets or other planetary systems? Did some of them do this?

RA: I am Ra. This is correct.

QUESTIONER: Then even though, from our point of view, there was great evolutionary experience, it was deemed at some point by the evolving Logos that an experiment to create a greater experience was appropriate. Is this correct?

RA: I am Ra. This is correct and may benefit from comment. The Logos is aware of the nature of the third-density requirement for what you have called graduation. All the previous, if you would use this term, experiments, although resulting in many experiences, lacked what was considered the crucial ingredient; that is, polarization. There was little enough tendency for experience to polarize entities that entities repeated habitually the third-density cycles many times over. It was desired that the potential for polarization be made more available.

QUESTIONER: Then since the only possibility at this particular time, as I see it, was a polarization for service-to-others, I must assume from what you said that even though all were aware of this service-to-others necessity, they were unable to achieve it. What was the configuration of mind of the mind/body/spirits at that time? Why did they have such a difficult time serving others to the extent necessary for graduation, since this was the only polarity possible?

RA: I am Ra. Consider, if you will, the tendency of those who are divinely happy, as you call this distortion, to have little urge to alter or better their condition. Such is the result of the mind/body/spirit which is not complex. There is the possibility of love of other-selves and service to other-selves, but there is the overwhelming awareness of the Creator in the self. The connection with the Creator is that of the umbilical cord. The security is total. Therefore, no love is terribly important; no pain terribly frightening; no effort, therefore, is made to serve for love or to benefit from fear.

QUESTIONER: It seems that you might make an analogy in our present illusion of those who are born into extreme wealth and security. Is this correct?

RA: I am Ra. Within the strict bounds of the simile, you are perceptive.

QUESTIONER: We have presently an activity between physical incarnations called the healing and review of the incarnation. Was anything of this nature occurring prior to the veil?

RA: I am Ra. The inchoate structure of this process was always in place, but where there has been no harm there need be no healing. This too may be seen to have been of concern to Logoi, which were aware that without the need to understand, understanding would forever be left undone. We ask your forgiveness for the use of this misnomer, but your language has a paucity of sound vibration complexes for this general concept.

QUESTIONER: I don't grasp too well the condition of incarnation and the time in between incarnations prior to the veil. I do not understand what was the difference other than the manifestation of the third-density, yellow-ray body. Was there any mental difference upon what we call death? I don't see the necessity for what we call the review of the incarnation if the consciousness was uninterrupted. Could you clear up that point for me?

RA: I am Ra. No portion of the Creator audits the course, to use your experiential terms. Each incarnation is intended to be a course in the Creator knowing Itself. A review or, shall we say, to continue the metaphor, each test is an integral portion of the process of the Creator knowing Itself. Each incarnation will end with such a test. This is so that the portion of the Creator may assimilate the experiences in yellow, physical, third density; may evaluate the biases gained; and may then choose, either by means of automatically provided aid or by the self, the conditions of the next incarnation.

QUESTIONER: Before the veil, during the review of the incarnation, were the entities at that time aware that what they were trying to do was sufficiently polarize for graduation?

RA: I am Ra. This is correct.

QUESTIONER: Then I am assuming that this awareness was somehow reduced as they went into the yellow-ray third-density incarnative state even though there was no veil. Is this correct?

RA: I am Ra. This is distinctly incorrect.

QUESTIONER: OK. This is the central important point. It seems to me that if polarization was the obvious thing that more effort would have been put forward to polarize. Let me see if I can state this differently. Before the veil there was an awareness of the need for polarization towards service to others in third density by all entities, whether incarnate in third-density, yellow-ray bodies or in between incarnations. I assume, then, that the condition of which we earlier spoke, one of wealth, you might say, was present through the entire spectrum of experience whether it might be between incarnations or during incarnations, and the entities just simply could not manifest the desire to create this polarization necessary for graduation. Is this correct?

RA: I am Ra. You begin to grasp the situation. Let us continue the metaphor of the schooling but consider the scholar as being an entity in your younger years of the schooling process. The entity is fed, clothed, and protected regardless of whether or not the schoolwork is accomplished. Therefore, the entity does not do the homework but rather enjoys playtime, mealtime, and vacation. It is not until there is a reason to wish to excel that most entities will attempt to excel.

QUESTIONER: You have stated in a much-earlier session that it is necessary to polarize more than 50 percent service to others to be harvestable fourth-density positive. Was this condition the same at the time before the veil?

RA: I am Ra. This shall be the last full query of this working.

The query is not answered easily, for the concept of service to self did not hold sway previous to what we have been calling the veiling process. The necessity for graduation to fourth density is an ability to use, welcome, and enjoy a certain intensity of the white light of the One Infinite Creator. In your own terms at your space/time nexus, this ability may be measured by your previously stated percentages of service.

Prior to the veiling process the measurement would be that of an entity walking up a set of your stairs, each of which was imbued with a certain quality of light. The stair upon which an entity stopped would be either third-density light or fourth-density light. Between the two stairs lies the threshold. To cross that threshold is difficult. There is resistance at the edge, shall we say, of each density. The faculty of faith or will needs to be understood, nourished, and developed in order to have an entity which seeks past the boundary of third density. Those entities which do not do their homework, be they ever so amiable, shall not cross. It was this situation which faced the Logoi prior to the veiling process being introduced into the experiential continuum of third density.

May we ask if there are any brief queries at this working?

QUESTIONER: Is there anything that we can do to improve the contact or make the instrument more comfortable?

RA: I am Ra. All parameters are being met. Remain united in love and thanksgiving. We thank you for your conscientiousness as regards the appurtenances.

I am Ra. I leave you in the love and in the light of the One Infinite Glorious Creator. Go forth, therefore, rejoicing merrily in the power and the peace of the One Creator. Adonai.

Session 83,
April 5, 1982

RA: I am Ra. I greet you in the love and in the light of the One Infinite Creator. I communicate now.

QUESTIONER: Could you first please give me the condition of the instrument?

RA: I am Ra. It is as previously stated.

QUESTIONER: Could you please tell me why the instrument now gains weight after a session instead of losing it?

RA: I am Ra. To assume that the instrument is gaining the weight of the physical bodily complex due to a session or working with Ra is erroneous. The instrument has no longer any physical material which, to any observable extent, must be used in order for this contact to occur. This is due to the determination of the group that the instrument shall not use the vital energy which would be necessary, since the physical-energy-complex level is in deficit. Since the energy, therefore, for these contacts is a product of energy transfer, the instrument must no longer pay this physical price. Therefore, the instrument is not losing the weight.

However, the weight gain, as it occurs, is the product of two factors. One is the increasing sensitivity of this physical vehicle to all that is placed before it, including that towards which it is distorted in ways you would call allergic. The second factor is the energizing of these difficulties.

It is fortunate for the outlook of this contact and the incarnation of this entity that it is not distorted towards the overeating, as the overloading of this much distorted physical complex would override even the most fervent affirmation of health/illness and turn the instrument towards the distortions of illness/health or, in the extreme case, the physical death.

QUESTIONER: Thank you. I'm going to ask a rather long, complex question, and I would request that the answer to each portion of this question be given if there was a significant difference prior to the veil than following the veil, so that I can get an idea of how what we experience now is used for better polarization.

What was the difference before the veil in the following while incarnate in third density: sleep, dreams, physical pain, mental pain, sex, disease, catalyst programming, random catalyst, relationships, and communication with the Higher Self or with the mind/body/spirit totality or any other mind, body, or spirit functions before the veil that would be significant with respect to their difference after the veil?

RA: I am Ra. Firstly, let us establish that both before and after the veil, the same conditions existed in time/space; that is, the veiling process is a space/time phenomenon.

Secondly, the character of experience was altered drastically by the veiling process. In some cases, such as the dreaming and the contact with the Higher Self, the experience was quantitatively different due to the fact that the veiling is a primary cause of the value of dreams and is also the single door against which the Higher Self must stand awaiting entry. Before veiling, dreams were not for the purpose of using the so-called unconscious to further utilize catalyst but were used to learn/teach from teach/learners within the inner planes as well as those of outer origins of higher density. As you deal with each subject of which you spoke, you may observe, during the veiling process, not a quantitative change in the experience but a qualitative one.

Let us, as an example, choose your sexual activities of energy transfer. If you have a desire to treat other subjects in detail, please query forthwith. In the instance of the sexual activity of those not dwelling within the veiling, each activity was a transfer. There were some transfers of strength. Most were rather attenuated in the strength of the transfer due to the lack of veiling.

In the third density, entities are attempting to learn the ways of love. If it can be seen that all are one being, it becomes much more difficult for the undisciplined personality to choose one mate and, thereby, initiate itself into a program of service. It is much more likely that the sexual energy will be dissipated more randomly without either great joy or great sorrow depending from these experiences.

Therefore, the green-ray energy transfer, being almost without exception the case in sexual energy transfer prior to veiling, remains weakened and without significant crystallization. The sexual energy transfers and blockages after veiling have been discussed previously. It may be seen to be a more complex study, but one far more efficient in crystallizing those who seek the green-ray energy center.

QUESTIONER: Let's take, then, since we are on the subject of sex, the relationship before and after the veil of disease, in this particular case venereal disease. Was this type of disease in existence prior to the veil?

RA: I am Ra. There has been that which is called disease, both of this type and others, before and after this great experiment. However, since the venereal disease is in large part a function of the thought-forms of a distorted nature which are associated with sexual energy blockage, the venereal disease is almost entirely the product of mind/body/spirit complexes' interaction after the veiling.

QUESTIONER: You mentioned that it existed in a small way prior to the veil. What was the source of its development prior to the veiling process?

RA: I am Ra. The source was as random as the nature of disease distortions are, at heart, in general. Each portion of the body complex is in a state of growth at all times. The reversal of this is seen as disease and has the benign function of ending an incarnation at the appropriate space/time nexus. This was the nature of disease, including that which you call venereal.

QUESTIONER: I'll make this statement and you can correct me. As I see the nature of the action of disease before the veil, it seems to me that the Logos had decided upon a program where an individual mind/body/spirit would continue to grow in mind, and the body would be the third-density analog of this mind. The growth would be continual unless there was an inability, for some reason, for the mind to continue along the growth patterns. If this growth decelerated or stopped, what we call disease would then act in a way so as to eventually terminate this physical experience so that a new physical experience would be started, after a review of the entire process had taken place between incarnations. Would you clear up my thinking on that, please?

RA: I am Ra. Your thinking is sufficiently clear on this subject.

QUESTIONER: The thing I don't understand is why, if there was no veil, the review of the incarnation after the incarnation would help the process, since it seems to me that the entity should already be aware of what was happening. Possibly this has to do with the nature of space/time and time/space. Could you clear that up, please?

RA: I am Ra. It is true that the nature of time/space is such that a lifetime may be seen whole as a book or record, the pages studied, riffled through, and reread. However, the value of review is that of the testing as opposed to the studying. At the testing, when the test is true, the distillations of all study are made clear. During the process of study, which you may call the incarnation, regardless of an entity's awareness of the process taking place, the material is diffused and overattention is almost inevitably placed upon detail.

The testing upon the cessation of the incarnative state is not that testing which involves the correct memorization of many details. This testing is, rather, the observing of self by self, often with aid as we have said. In this observation one sees the sum of all the detailed study, that being an attitude or complex of attitudes which bias the consciousness of the mind/body/spirit.

QUESTIONER: Now, before the veil an entity would be aware that he was experiencing a disease. As an analogy would you give me, if you are aware of a case, a disease an entity might experience prior to the veil and how he would react to this and think about it and what effect it would have on him?

RA: I am Ra. Inasmuch as the universe is composed of an infinite array of entities, there is also an infinity of response to stimulus. If you will observe your peoples you will discover greatly variant responses to the same distortion towards disease. Consequently, we cannot answer your query with any hope of making any true statements, since the over-generalizations required are too capacious.

QUESTIONER: Was there any uniformity or like functions of societies or social organizations prior to the veil?

RA: I am Ra. The third density is, by its very fiber, a societal one. There are societies wherever there are entities conscious of the self and conscious of other-selves and possessed with intelligence adequate to process information indicating the benefits of communal blending of energies. The structures of society before as after veiling were various. However, the societies before veiling did not depend in any case upon the intentional enslavement of some for the benefit of others, this not being seen to be a possibility when all are seen as one. There was, however, the requisite amount of disharmony to produce various experiments in what you may call governmental or societal structures.

QUESTIONER: In our present illusion we have undoubtedly lost sight of the techniques of enslavement that are used, since we are so far departed from the pre-veil experience. I am sure that many of service-to-others orientation are using techniques of enslavement even though they are not aware that these are techniques of enslavement, simply because they have been evolved over so long a period of time and we are so deep into the illusion. Is this not correct?

RA: I am Ra. This is incorrect.

QUESTIONER: Then you say that there are no cases where those who are of a service-to-others orientation are using techniques of enslavement that have grown as a result of the evolution of our social structures? Is this what you mean?

RA: I am Ra. It was our understanding that your query concerned conditions before the veiling. There was no unconscious slavery, as you call this condition, at that period. At the present space/time the conditions of well-meant and unintentional slavery are so numerous that it beggars our ability to enumerate them.

QUESTIONER: Then for a service-to-others-oriented entity at this time, meditation upon the nature of these little-expected forms of slavery might be productive in polarization, I would think. Am I correct?

RA: I am Ra. You are quite correct.

QUESTIONER: I would say that a very high percentage of the laws and restrictions within what we call our legal system are of a nature of enslavement of which I just spoke. Would you agree with this?

RA: I am Ra. It is a necessary balance to the intention of law, which is to protect, that the result would encompass an equal distortion towards imprisonment. Therefore, we may say that your supposition is correct. This is not to denigrate those who, in green- and blue-ray energies, sought to free a peaceable people from the bonds of chaos, but only to point out the inevitable consequences of codification of response which does not recognize the uniqueness of each and every situation within your experience.

QUESTIONER: Is the veil supposed to be what I would call semipermeable?

RA: I am Ra. The veil is indeed so.

QUESTIONER: What techniques and methods of penetration of the veil were planned, and are there any others that have occurred other that those planned?

RA: I am Ra. There were none planned by the first great experiment. As all experiments, this rested upon the nakedness of hypothesis. The outcome was unknown. It was discovered, experientially and empirically, that there were as many ways to penetrate the veil as the imagination of mind/body/spirit complexes could provide. The desire of mind/body/spirit complexes to know that which was unknown drew to them the dreaming and the gradual opening to the seeker of all of the balancing mechanisms, leading to adepthood and communication with teach/learners which could pierce this veil.

The various unmanifested activities of the self were found to be productive in some degree of penetration of the veil. In general, we may say that by far the most vivid and even extravagant opportunities for the piercing of the veil are a result of the interaction of polarized entities.

QUESTIONER: Could you expand on what you mean by that interaction of polarized entities in piercing the veil?

RA: I am Ra. We shall state two items of note. The first is the extreme potential for polarization in the relationship of two polarized entities which have embarked upon the service-to-others path or, in some few cases, the service-to-self path. Secondly, we would note that effect which we have learned to call the doubling effect. Those of like mind which together seek shall far more surely find.

QUESTIONER: Specifically, by what process would, in the first case, two polarized entities attempt to penetrate the veil, whether they be positively or negatively polarized? By what technique would they penetrate the veil?

RA: I am Ra. The penetration of the veil may be seen to begin to have its roots in the gestation of green-ray activity, that all-compassionate love which demands no return. If this path is followed, the higher energy centers shall be activated and crystallized until the adept is born. Within the adept is the potential for dismantling the veil to a greater or lesser extent that all may be seen again as one. The other-self is primary catalyst in this particular path to the piercing of the veil, if you would call it that.

QUESTIONER: What was the mechanism of the very first veiling process? I don't know if you can answer that. Would you try to answer that?

RA: I am Ra. The mechanism of the veiling between the conscious and unconscious portions of the mind was a declaration that the mind was complex. This, in turn, caused the body and the spirit to become complex.

QUESTIONER: Would you give me an example of a complex activity of the body that we have now, and how it was not complex prior to the veil?

RA: I am Ra. Prior to the great experiment a mind/body/spirit was capable of controlling the pressure of blood in the veins, the beating of the organ you call the heart, the intensity of the sensation known to you as pain, and all the functions now understood to be involuntary or unconscious.

QUESTIONER: When the veiling process originally took place, then, it seems that the Logos must have had a list of those functions that would become unconscious and those that would remain consciously controlled. I am assuming that if this occurred, there was good reason for these divisions. Am I in any way correct on this?

RA: I am Ra. No.

QUESTIONER: Would you correct me, please?

RA: I am Ra. There were many experiments whereby various of the functions or distortions of the body complex were veiled and others not. A large number of these experiments resulted in nonviable body complexes or those only marginally viable. For instance, it is not a survival-oriented mechanism for the nerve receptors to blank out unconsciously any distortions towards pain.

QUESTIONER: Before the veil the mind could blank out pain. I assume, then, that the function of the pain at that time was to signal the body to assume a different configuration so that the source of the pain would leave, and then the pain could be eliminated mentally. Is that correct, and was there another function for the pain prior to the veiling?

RA: I am Ra. Your assumption is correct. The function of pain at that time was as the warning of the fire alarm to those not smelling the smoke.

QUESTIONER: Then let's say that an entity at that time burned its hand due to carelessness. It would immediately remove its hand from the burning object, and then, in order to not feel the pain any more, its mind would cut the pain off until healing had taken place. Is this correct?

RA: I am Ra. This is correct.

QUESTIONER: We would look at this in our present illusion as an elimination of a certain amount of catalyst that would produce an acceleration in our evolution. Is this correct?

RA: I am Ra. The attitude towards pain varies from mind/body/spirit complex to mind/body/spirit complex. Your verbalization of attitude towards the distortion known as pain is one productive of helpful distortions as regards the process of evolution.

QUESTIONER: What I was trying to indicate was that the plan of the Logos in veiling the conscious from the unconscious mind in such a way that pain could not so easily be controlled would have created a system of catalyst that was not previously usable. Is this generally correct?

RA: I am Ra. Yes.

QUESTIONER: In some cases it seems that this use of catalyst is almost in a runaway condition for some entities, in that they are experiencing much more pain than they can make good use of as far as catalytic nature would be considered. Could you comment on that?

RA: I am Ra. This shall be the last query of this working of a full length. You may see, in some cases, an entity which, either by pre-incarnative choice or by constant reprogramming while in incarnation, has developed an esurient program of catalyst. Such an entity is quite desirous of using the catalyst and has determined to its own satisfaction that what you may call the large board needs to be applied to the forehead in order to obtain the attention of the self. In these cases it may indeed seem a great waste of the catalyst of pain and a distortion towards feeling the tragedy of so much pain may be experienced by the other-self. However, it is well to hope that the other-self is grasping that which it has gone to some trouble to offer itself; that is, the catalyst which it desires to use for the purpose of evolution. May we ask if there are any brief queries at this time?

QUESTIONER: I noticed you started this session with "I communicate now," and you usually use "We communicate now." Is there any significance or difference with respect to that, and then is there anything that we can do to make the instrument more comfortable or to improve the contact?

RA: I am Ra. We am Ra. You may see the grammatical difficulties of your linguistic structure in dealing with a social memory complex. There is no distinction between the first-person singular and plural in your language when pertaining to Ra.

We offer the following, not to infringe upon your free will, but because this instrument has specifically requested information as to its maintenance, and the support group does so at this querying. We may suggest that the instrument has two areas of potential distortion, both of which may be aided in the bodily sense by the ingestion of those things which seem to the instrument to be desirable. We do not suggest any hard-and-fast rulings of diet, although we may suggest the virtue of the liquids. The instrument has an increasing ability to sense that which will aid its bodily complex. It is being aided by affirmations and also by the light which is the food of the density of resting.

We may ask the support group to monitor the instrument as always, so that in the case of the desire for the more complex proteins, that which is the least distorted might be offered to the bodily complex which is indeed at this time potentially capable of greatly increased distortion.

I am Ra. We thank you, my friends, for your continued conscientiousness in the fulfilling of your manifestation of desire to serve others. You are conscientious. The appurtenances are quite well aligned.

I am Ra. I leave you, my friends, in the love and in the light of the One Infinite Creator. Go forth, therefore, rejoicing merrily in the power and in the peace of the One Infinite Creator. Adonai.

Session 84,
April 14, 1982

RA: I am Ra. I greet you, my friends, in the love and in the light of the One Infinite Creator. We communicate now.

QUESTIONER: Could you first please give me the condition of the instrument?

RA: I am Ra. The physical-complex energy level of the instrument is in sizable deficit. The vital energies are well.

QUESTIONER: In the last session you mentioned the least distorted complex protein for the instrument since its body complex was capable of greatly increased distortion. Would you define the protein of which you spoke, and in which direction is the increased distortion, towards health or ill health?

RA: I am Ra. We were, in the cautionary statement about complex protein, referring to the distortions of the animal protein which has been slaughtered and preservatives added in order to maintain the acceptability to your peoples of this nonliving, physical material. It is well to attempt to find those items which are fresh and of the best quality possible in order to avoid increasing this particular entity's distortions which may be loosely termed allergic.

We were speaking of the distortion towards disease which is potential at this space/time.

QUESTIONER: The instrument asked the following question: Ra has implied that the instrument is on the path of martyrdom, but since we all die, are we not all martyred to something, and when, if ever, does martyrdom partake of wisdom?

RA: I am Ra. This is a thoughtful query. Let us use as exemplar the one known as Jehoshua. This entity incarnated with the plan of martyrdom. There is no wisdom in this plan, but rather understanding and compassion extended to its fullest perfection. The one known as Jehoshua would have been less than fully understanding of its course had it chosen to follow its will at any space/time during its teachings. Several times, as you call this measure, this entity had the possibility of moving towards the martyr's place which was, for that martyr, Jerusalem. Yet, in meditation this entity stated, time and again, "It is not yet the hour." The entity could also have, when the hour came, walked another path. Its incarnation would then have been prolonged, but the path for which it incarnated somewhat confused. Thusly, one may observe the greatest amount of understanding, of which this entity was indeed capable, taking place as the entity in meditation felt and knew that the hour had come for that to be fulfilled which was its incarnation.

It is indeed so that all mind/body/spirit complexes shall die to the third-density illusion; that is, that each yellow-ray physical-complex body shall cease to be viable. It is a misnomer to, for this reason alone, call each mind/body/spirit complex a martyr, for this term is reserved for those who lay down their lives for the service they may provide to others. We may encourage meditation upon the functions of the will.

QUESTIONER: The instrument asked if the restricted, unpublishable healing information that was given during the first book could be included in Book IV, since readers who have gotten that far will be dedicated somewhat?

RA: I am Ra. This publication of material shall, in time, shall we say, be appropriate. There is intervening material.

QUESTIONER: Going back to the previous session, you stated that each sexual activity was a transfer before the veil. Would you trace the flow of energy that is transferred and tell me if that was the planned activity or a planned transfer by the designing Logos?

RA: I am Ra. The path of energy transfer before the veiling during the sexual intercourse was that of the two entities possessed of green-ray capability. The awareness of all as Creator is that which opens the green energy center. Thusly there was no possibility of blockage due to the sure knowledge of each by each that each was the Creator. The transfers were weak due to the ease with which such transfers could take place between any two polarized entities during sexual intercourse.

QUESTIONER: What I was getting at, precisely, was, for example, when we close an electrical circuit it is easy to trace the path of current. It goes along the conductor. I am trying to determine whether this transfer is between the green energy centers (the heart chakras). I am trying to trace the physical flow of the energy to try to get an idea of blockages after the veil. I may be off on the wrong track here, but if I am wrong we'll just drop it. Can you tell me something about that?

RA: I am Ra. In such a drawing or schematic representation of the circuitry of two mind/body/spirits or mind/body/spirit complexes in sexual or other energy transfer, the circuit opens always at the red or base center and moves as possible through the intervening energy centers. If baffled, it will stop at orange. If not, it shall proceed to yellow. If still unbaffled, it shall proceed to green. It is well to remember in the case of the mind/body/spirit that the chakras or energy centers could well be functioning without crystallization.

QUESTIONER: In other words, they would be functioning, but it would be equivalent in an electrical circuitry to having a high resistance, shall we say, and although the circuit would be complete, red through green, the total quantity of energy transferred would be less. Is this correct?

RA: I am Ra. We might most closely associate your query with the concept of voltage. The uncrystallized, lower centers cannot deliver the higher voltage. The crystallized centers may become quite remarkable in the high-voltage characteristics of the energy transfer as it reaches green ray, and indeed as green ray is crystallized this also applies to the higher energy centers until such energy transfers become an honestation[4] for the Creator.

QUESTIONER: Would you please correct me on this statement. I am guessing that what happens is that when a transfer takes place, the energy is that light energy that comes in through the feet of the entity, and the voltage or potential difference is measured between the red energy center and, in the case of the green-ray transfer, the green energy center and then must leap or flow from the green energy center of one entity to the green energy center of the other, and then something happens to it. Could you clarify my thinking on that?

RA: I am Ra. Yes.

QUESTIONER: Would you please do that?

RA: I am Ra. The energy transfer occurs in one releasing of the potential difference. This does not leap between green and green energy centers but is the sharing of the energies of each from red ray upwards. In this context it may be seen to be at its most efficient when both entities have orgasm simultaneously. However, it functions as transfer if either has the orgasm, and indeed in the case of the physically expressed love between a mated pair which does not have the conclusion you call orgasm, there is, nonetheless, a considerable amount of energy transferred due to the potential difference which has been raised as long as both entities are aware of this potential and release its strength to each other by desire of the will in a mental or mind complex dedication. You may see this practice as being used to generate energy transfers in some of your practices of what you may call other than Christian religious-distortion systems of the Law of One.

QUESTIONER: Could you give me an example of that last statement?

---

4. honestation: n. adornment; grace. [obs.]

RA: I am Ra. We preface this example with the reminder that each system is quite distorted, and its teachings always half lost. However, one such system is that called the tantric yoga.

QUESTIONER: Considering individual A and individual B, if individual A experiences the orgasm, is the energy, then, transferred to individual B in a greater amount? Is that correct?

RA: I am Ra. Your query is incomplete. Please restate.

QUESTIONER: I am trying to determine whether the direction of energy transfer is a function of orgasm. Which entity gets the transferred energy? I know it's a dumb question, but I want to be sure that I have it cleared up.

RA: I am Ra. If both entities are well polarized and vibrating in green-ray love, any orgasm shall offer equal energy to both.

QUESTIONER: I see. Before the veil, can you describe any other physical difference that we haven't talked about yet with respect to the sexual energy transfers or relationships or anything prior to veiling?

RA: I am Ra. Perhaps the most critical difference of the veiling, before and after, was that before the mind, body, and spirit were veiled, entities were aware that each energy transfer and, indeed, very nearly all that proceeds from any intercourse, social or sexual, between two entities has its character and substance in time/space rather than space/time. The energies transferred during the sexual activity are not, properly speaking, of space/time. There is a great component of what you may call metaphysical energy transferred. Indeed, the body complex as a whole is greatly misunderstood due to the post-veiling assumption that the physical manifestation called the body is subject only to physical stimuli. This is emphatically not so.

QUESTIONER: After the veil, in our particular case now, we have, in the circuitry of which we were speaking, what you call blockages. Could you describe what occurs with the first blockage and what its effects are on each of the entities, assuming that one blocks and the other does not, or if both are blocked?

RA: I am Ra. This material has been covered previously. If both entities are blocked, both will have an increased hunger for the same activity, seeking to unblock the baffled flow of energy. If one entity is blocked and the other vibrates in love, the entity baffled will hunger still but have a tendency to attempt to continue the procedure of satiating the increasing hunger with the one vibrating green ray, due to an impression that this entity might prove helpful in this endeavor. The green-ray-active individual shall polarize slightly in the direction of service to others but have only the energy with which it began.

QUESTIONER: I didn't mean to cover previously covered material. What I was actually attempting to do was discover something new in asking the question, so please, if I ask any questions in the future that have already been covered, don't bother to repeat the material. I am just searching the same area for the possibility of greater enlightenment with respect to this particular area, since it seems to be one of the major areas of experience in our present condition of veiling that produces a very large amount of catalyst, and I am trying to understand, to use a poor term, how this veiling process created a greater experience and how this experience evolved. These questions are very difficult to ask.

It occurs to me that many statues or drawings of the one known as Lucifer or the Devil are shown with an erection. Is this a function of orange-ray blockage, and was this known in a minimal way by those who devised these statues and drawings?

RA: I am Ra. There is, of course, much other distortion involved in a discussion of any mythic archetypical form. However, we may answer in the affirmative and note that you are perceptive.

QUESTIONER: With respect to the green, blue, and indigo transfers of energy, how would the mechanism for these transfers differ from the orange-ray mechanism in making them possible or setting the groundwork for them? I know this is very difficult to ask, and I may not be making any sense, but what I am trying to do is gain an understanding of the foundation for the transfers in each of the rays, and the preparations for the transfers or the fundamental requirements or biases and potentials for these transfers. Could you expand on that for me, please? I am sorry for the poor question.

RA: I am Ra. We would take a moment to state in reply to a previous comment that we shall answer each query whether or not it has been previously covered, for not to do so would be to baffle the flow of quite another transfer of energy.

To respond to your query, we firstly wish to agree with your supposition that the subject you now query upon is a large one, for in it lies an entire system of opening the gateway to intelligent infinity. You may see that some information is necessarily shrouded in mystery by our desire to preserve the free will of the adept. The great key to blue, indigo, and, finally, that great capital of the column of sexual energy transfer, violet energy transfers, is the metaphysical bond or distortion which has the name among your peoples of unconditional love. In the blue-ray energy transfer the quality of this love is refined in the fire of honest communication and clarity; this, shall we say, normally speaking in general, takes a substantial portion of your space/time to accomplish, although there are instances of matings so well refined in previous incarnations and so well remembered that the blue ray may be penetrated at once. This energy transfer is of great benefit to the seeker in that all communication from this seeker is, thereby, refined and the eyes of honesty and clarity look upon a new world. Such is the nature of blue-ray energy, and such is one mechanism of potentiating and crystallizing it.

As we approach indigo-ray transfer, we find ourselves in a shadowland. We cannot give you information straight out or plain, for this is seen by us to be an infringement. We cannot speak at all of violet-ray transfer as we do not, again, desire to break the Law of Confusion.

We may say that these jewels, though dearly bought, are beyond price for the seeker and might suggest that just as each awareness is arrived at through a process of analysis, synthesis, and inspiration, so should the seeker approach its mate and evaluate each experience, seeking the jewel.

QUESTIONER: Is there any way to tell which ray the transfer was for an individual after the experience?

RA: I am Ra. There is only a subjective yardstick or measure of such. If the energies have flowed so that love is made whole, green-ray transfer has taken place. If, by the same entities' exchange, greater ease in communication and greater sight has been experienced, the energy has been refined to the blue-ray energy center. If the polarized entities, by this same energy transfer experience, find that the faculties of will and faith have been stimulated, not for a brief while but for a great duration of what you call time, you may perceive the indigo-ray transfer. We may not speak of the violet-ray transfer except to note that it is an opening to the gateway of intelligent infinity. Indeed, the indigo-ray transfer is also this, but, shall we say, the veil has not yet been lifted.

QUESTIONER: Did most Logoi plan, before the veil, to create a system of random sexual activity or the specific pairing of entities for specific periods of time, or did they have an objective in this respect?

RA: I am Ra. This shall be the last full query of this working.

The harvest from the previous creation was that which included the male and female mind/body/spirit. It was the intention of the original Logoi that entities mate with one another in any fashion which caused a greater polarization. It was determined, after observation of the process of many Logoi, that polarization increased manyfold if the mating were not indiscriminate. Consequent Logoi thusly preserved a bias towards the mated relationship which is more characteristic of more-disciplined personalities and of what you may call higher densities. The free will of each entity, however, was always paramount, and a bias only could be offered.

May we ask if there may be any brief queries before we leave this instrument?

QUESTIONER: Is there any way that we can make the instrument more comfortable or to improve the contact?

RA: I am Ra. We would ask that each of the support group be especially vigilant in the, what you would call, immediate future due to this instrument's unbidden but serious potential for increased distortion towards illness/health.

You are most conscientious. We thank you, my friends, and leave you in the glorious light and love of the One Infinite Creator. Go forth, therefore, rejoicing in the power and in the peace of the One Infinite Creator. Adonai.

Session 85,
April 26, 1982

RA: I am Ra. We communicate now.

QUESTIONER: Could you first give me the condition of the instrument?

RA: I am Ra. We ask your permission to preface this answer by the inclusion of the greeting which we use.

QUESTIONER: That is agreeable.

RA: I am Ra. We greet you in the love and in the light of the One Infinite Creator. We were having some difficulty with the channel of energy influx due to pain flare, as you call this distortion of the physical-body complex of this instrument. Therefore, it was necessary to speak as briefly as possible until we had safely transferred the mind/body/spirit complex of this instrument. We beg your kind indulgence for our discourtesy, which was appropriate.

The condition of this instrument is as follows. The necessity for extreme vigilance is less, due to the somewhat lessened physical-complex energy deficit. The potential for distortion remains, and continued watchfulness over the ingestion of helpful foodstuffs continues to be recommended. Although the instrument is experiencing more than the, shall we say, normal, for this mind/body/spirit complex, distortions towards pain at this space/time nexus, the basic condition is less distorted. The vital energies are as previously stated.

We commend the vigilance and care of this group.

QUESTIONER: What is the current situation with respect to our fifth-density, service-to-self polarized companion?

RA: I am Ra. Your companion has never been more closely associated with you than at the present nexus. You may see a kind of crisis occurring upon the so-called magical level at this particular space/time nexus.

QUESTIONER: What is the nature of this crisis?

RA: I am Ra. The nature of this crisis is the determination of the relative polarity of your companion and your selves. You are in the position of being in the third-density illusion and consequently having the conscious collective magical ability of the neophyte, whereas your companion is most adept. However, the faculties of will and faith and the calling to the light have been used by this group to the exclusion of any significant depolarization from the service-to-others path.

If your companion can possibly depolarize this group, it must do so and that quickly, for in this unsuccessful attempt at exploring the wisdom of separation, it is encountering some depolarization. This shall continue. Therefore, the efforts of your companion are pronounced at this space/time and time/space nexus.

QUESTIONER: I am totally aware of the lack of necessity or rational need for naming of entities or things, but I was wondering if this particular entity had a name, just so that we could increase our efficiency of communicating with respect to him. Does he have a name?

RA: I am Ra. Yes.

QUESTIONER: Would it be magically bad for us to know that name, or would it make no difference?

RA: I am Ra. It would make a difference.

QUESTIONER: What would the difference be?

RA: I am Ra. If one wishes to have power over an entity, it is an aid to know that entity's name. If one wishes no power over an entity but wishes to collect that entity into the very heart of one's own being, it is well to forget the naming. Both processes are magically viable. Each is polarized in a specific way. It is your choice.

QUESTIONER: I am assuming that it would be a problem for the instrument to meditate without the hand pressure from the other-self at this time because of the continued greeting. Is this correct?

RA: I am Ra. This is correct if the instrument wishes to remain free from this potential separation of its mind/body/spirit complex from the third density it now experiences.

QUESTIONER: Since our fifth-density companion has been monitoring our communication with Ra, it has been made aware of the veiling process of which we have been speaking. It seems to me that conscious knowledge and acceptance of the fact that this veiling process was used for the purpose for which it was used would make it difficult to maintain high negative polarization. Could you clear up my thinking on that, please?

RA: I am Ra. We are unsure as to our success in realigning your modes of mentation. We may, however, comment.

The polarization process, as it enters fourth density, is one which occurs with full knowledge of the veiling process which has taken place in third density. This veiling process is that which is a portion of the third-density experience. The knowledge and memory of the outcome of this and all portions of the third-density experience informs the higher-density polarized entity. It, however, does not influence the choice which has been made and which is the basis for further work past third density in polarization. Those which have chosen the service-to-others (self)[5] path have simply used the veiling process in order to potentiate that which is not. This is an entirely acceptable method of self-knowledge of and by the Creator.

QUESTIONER: You just stated that those who are on the service-to-others path use the veiling process to potentiate that which is not. I believe that I am correct in repeating what you said. Is that correct?

RA: I am Ra. Yes.

QUESTIONER: Then the service-to-others path has potentiated that which is not. Could you expand that a little bit so that I could understand it a little better?

RA: I am Ra. If you see the energy centers in their various colors completing the spectrum, you may see that the service-to-others (self)[5] choice is one which denies the very center of the spectrum, that being universal love. Therefore, all that is built upon the penetration of the light of harvestable quality by such entities is based upon an omission. This omission shall manifest in fourth density as the love of self; that is, the fullest expression of the orange and yellow energy centers, which then are used to potentiate communication and adepthood.

When fifth-density refinement has been achieved, that which is not is carried further, the wisdom density being explored by entities which have no compassion, no universal love. They experience that which they wish by free choice, being of the earnest opinion that green-ray energy is folly.

That which is not may be seen as a self-imposed darkness in which harmony is turned into an eternal disharmony. However, that which is not cannot endure throughout the octave of third density, and, as darkness eventually calls the light, so does that which is not eventually call that which is.

QUESTIONER: I believe that there were salient errors in the communication that we just completed because of transmission difficulties. Are you aware of these errors?

RA: I am Ra. We are unaware of errors, although this instrument is

---

5. Ra corrects this error in the next two answers.

experiencing flares of pain, as you call this distortion. We welcome and encourage your perceptions in correcting any errors in transmission.

QUESTIONER: I think that the statement that was made when we were speaking about the service-to-others path was incorrect. Would you check that, please?

RA: I am Ra. May we ask that you be apprised of our intention to have spoken of the service-to-self path as the path of that which is not.

QUESTIONER: I am interested in the problem that we sometimes have with the transmission, since the word "others" was used three times in this transmission rather than the word "self." Could you give me an idea of this problem which could create a discrepancy in communication?

RA: I am Ra. Firstly, we may note the clumsiness of language and our unfamiliarity with it in our native, shall we say, experience. Secondly, we may point out that once we have miscalled or misnumbered an event or thing, that referent is quite likely to be reused for some transmission time, as you call this measurement, due to our original error having gone undetected by ourselves.

QUESTIONER: Thank you. Do you have use of all the words in the English language and, for that matter, all of the words in all of the languages that are spoken on this planet at this time?

RA: I am Ra. No.

QUESTIONER: I have a question here from [name]. It states: "As we see compassion developing in ourselves, is it more appropriate to balance this compassion with wisdom or to allow the compassion to develop as much as possible without being balanced?"

RA: I am Ra. This query borders upon that type of question to which answers are unavailable due to the free-will prohibitions upon information from teach/learners.

To the student of the balancing process, we may suggest that the most stringent honesty be applied. As compassion is perceived, it is suggested that, in balancing, this perception be analyzed. It may take many, many essays into compassion before true universal love is the product of the attempted opening and crystallization of this all-important springboard energy center. Thus the student may discover many other components to what may seem to be all-embracing love. Each of these components may be balanced and accepted as part of the self and as transitional material as the entity's seat of learn/teaching moves ever more clearly into the green ray.

When it is perceived that universal love has been achieved, the next balancing may or may not be wisdom. If the adept is balancing manifestations, it is indeed appropriate to balance universal love and wisdom. If the balancing is of mind or spirit, there are many subtleties to which the adept may give careful consideration. Love and wisdom, like love and light, are not black and white, shall we say, but faces of the same coin, if you will. Therefore, it is not, in all cases, that balancing consists of a movement from compassion to wisdom.

We may suggest at all times the constant remembrance of the density from which each adept desires to move. This density learns the lessons of love. In the case of Wanderers, there are half-forgotten overlays of other lessons and other densities. We shall leave these considerations with the questioner and invite observations which we shall then be most happy to respond to in what may seem to be a more effectual manner.

QUESTIONER: What changes of functions of the mind/body/spirits were most effective in producing the evolution desired due to the veiling process?

RA: I am Ra. We are having difficulty retaining clear channel through this instrument. It has a safe margin of transferred energy but is experiencing pain flares. May we ask that you repeat the query, as we have better channel now.

QUESTIONER: After the veiling process, certain veiled functions or activities must have been paramount in creating evolution in the desired polarized directions. I was just wondering which of these had the greatest effect on polarization.

RA: I am Ra. The most effectual veiling was that of the mind.

QUESTIONER: I would like to carry that on to find out what specific functions of the mind were most effectual, and the three or four most effective changes brought about to create the polarization.

RA: I am Ra. This is an interesting query. The primary veiling was of such significance that it may be seen to be analogous to the mantling of the Earth over all the jewels within the Earth's crust, whereas previously, all facets of the Creator were consciously known. After the veiling, almost no facets of the Creator were known to the mind. Almost all was buried beneath the veil.

If one were to attempt to list those functions of mind most significant, in that they might be of aid in polarization, one would need to begin with the faculty of visioning, envisioning, or far-seeing. Without the veil the mind was not caught in your illusory time. With the veil, space/time is the only obvious possibility for experience.

Also upon the list of significant veiled functions of the mind would be that of dreaming. The so-called dreaming contains a great deal which, if made available to the conscious mind and used, shall aid it in polarization to a great extent.

The third function of the mind which is significant and which has been veiled is that of the knowing of the body. The knowledge of and control over the body, having been lost to a great extent in the veiling process, is thusly lost from the experience of the seeker. Its knowledge before the veiling is of small use. Its knowledge after the veiling, and in the face of what is now a dense illusion of separation of body complex from mind complex, is quite significant.

Perhaps the most important and significant function that occurred due to the veiling of the mind from itself is not in itself a function of mind but rather is a product of the potential created by this veiling. This is the faculty of will or pure desire.

We may ask for brief queries at this time. Although there is energy remaining for this working, we are reluctant to continue this contact, experiencing continual variations due to pain flares, as you call this distortion. Although we are unaware of any misgiven material, we are aware that there have been several points during which our channel was less than optimal. This instrument is most faithful, but we do not wish to misuse this instrument. Please query as you will.

QUESTIONER: I will just ask in closing: is an individualized portion or entity of Ra inhabiting the instrument's body for the purpose of communication? Then, is there anything that we could do to improve the contact or to make the instrument more comfortable?

RA: I am Ra. We of Ra communicate through narrow band channel through the violet-ray energy center. We are not, as you would say, physically indwelling in this instrument; rather, the mind/body/spirit complex of this instrument rests with us.

You are diligent and conscientious. The alignments are excellent. We leave you rejoicing in the power and in the peace of the One

Infinite Creator. Go forth, then, my friends, rejoicing in the power and in the peace of the infinite love and the ineffable light of the One Creator. I am Ra. Adonai.

Session 86,
May 4, 1982

RA: I am Ra. I greet you in the love and in the light of the One Infinite Creator. We communicate now.

QUESTIONER: Would you first please give me the condition of the instrument?

RA: I am Ra. The instrument's distortion towards physical-energy-complex deficit has slightly increased since the last asking. The vital energy levels have had significant calls upon them and are somewhat less than the last asking also.

QUESTIONER: What was the nature of the significant calls upon the vital energy?

RA: I am Ra. There are those entities which entertain the thought distortion towards this entity that it shall remove for the other selves all distortions for the other-self. This entity has recently been in close contact with a larger-than-normal number of entities with these thought complex distortions. This entity is of the distortion to provide whatever service is possible and is not consciously aware of the inroads made upon the vital energies.

QUESTIONER: Am I correct in assuming that you are speaking of incarnate third-density entities that were creating the condition of the use of the vital energy?

RA: I am Ra. Yes.

QUESTIONER: What is the present situation with our fifth-density service-to-self polarized companion?

RA: I am Ra. The period which you may call crisis remains.

QUESTIONER: Can you tell me anything of the nature of this crisis?

RA: I am Ra. The polarity of your companion is approaching the critical point at which the entity shall choose either to retreat for the nonce and leave any greetings to fourth-density minions or lose polarity. The only other potential is that in some way this group might lose polarity, in which case your companion could continue its form of greeting.

QUESTIONER: In the last session you had mentioned the properties precipitating from the veiling of the mind, the first being envisioning or far-seeing. Would you explain the meaning of that?

RA: I am Ra. Your language is not overstrewn with non-emotional terms for the functional qualities of what is now termed unconscious mind. The nature of mind is something which we have requested that you ponder. However, it is, shall we say, clear enough to the casual observer that we may share some thoughts with you without infringing upon your free learn/teaching experiences.

The nature of the unconscious is of the nature of concept rather than word. Consequently, before the veiling the use of the deeper mind was that of the use of unspoken concept. You may consider the emotive and connotative aspects of a melody. One could call out, in some stylized fashion, the terms for the notes of the melody. One could say, quarter note A, quarter note A, quarter note A, whole note F. This bears little resemblance to the beginning of the melody of one of your composer's most influential melodies, that known to you as a symbol of victory.

This is the nature of the deeper mind. There are only stylized methods with which to discuss its functions. Thusly our descriptions of this portion of the mind, as well as the same portions of body and spirit, were given terms such as "far-seeing," indicating that the nature of penetration of the veiled portion of the mind may be likened unto the journey too rich and exotic to contemplate adequate describing thereof.

QUESTIONER: You have stated that dreaming, if made available to the conscious mind, will aid greatly in polarization. Could you define dreaming or tell us what it is and how it aids polarization?

RA: I am Ra. Dreaming is an activity of communication through the veil of the unconscious mind and the conscious mind. The nature of this activity is wholly dependent upon the situation regarding the energy center blockages, activations, and crystallizations of a given mind/body/spirit complex.

In one who is blocked at two of the three lower energy centers, dreaming will be of value in the polarization process in that there will be a repetition of those portions of recent catalyst as well as deeper-held blockages, thereby giving the waking mind clues as to the nature of these blockages, and hints as to possible changes in perception which may lead to the unblocking.

This type of dreaming or communication through the veiled portions of the mind occurs also with those mind/body/spirit complexes which are functioning with far less blockage and enjoying the green-ray activation or higher activation at those times at which the mind/body/spirit complex experiences catalyst, momentarily reblocking or baffling or otherwise distorting the flow of energy influx. Therefore, in all cases it is useful to a mind/body/spirit complex to ponder the content and emotive resonance of dreams.

For those whose green-ray energy centers have been activated, as well as for those whose green-ray energy centers are offered an unusual unblockage due to extreme catalyst, such as what is termed the physical death of the self or one which is beloved occurring in what you may call your near future, dreaming takes on another activity. This is what may loosely be termed precognition or a knowing which is prior to that which shall occur in physical manifestation in your yellow-ray, third- density space/time. This property of the mind depends upon its placement, to a great extent, in time/space, so that the terms of present and future and past have no meaning. This will, if made proper use of by the mind/body/spirit complex, enable this entity to enter more fully into the all-compassionate love of each and every circumstance, including those circumstances against which an entity may have a strong distortion towards what you may call unhappiness.

As a mind/body/spirit complex consciously chooses the path of the adept and, with each energy balanced to a minimal degree, begins to open the indigo-ray energy center, the so-called dreaming becomes the most efficient tool for polarization, for, if it is known by the adept that work may be done in consciousness while the so-called conscious mind rests, this adept may call upon those which guide it, those presences which surround it, and, most of all, the magical personality, which is the Higher Self in space/time analog as it moves into the sleeping mode of consciousness. With these affirmations attended to, the activity of dreaming reaches that potential of learn/teaching which is most helpful to increasing the distortions of the adept towards its chosen polarity.

There are other possibilities of the dreaming not so closely aligned with the increase in polarity, which we do not cover at this particular space/time.

QUESTIONER: How is the dream designed or programmed? Is it done by the Higher Self, or who is responsible for this?

RA: I am Ra. In all cases the mind/body/spirit complex makes what use it can of the faculty of the dreaming. It, itself, is responsible for this activity.

QUESTIONER: Then you are saying that the subconscious is responsible for what I will call the design or scriptwriter for the dream. Is this correct?

RA: I am Ra. This is correct.

QUESTIONER: Is the memory that the individual has upon waking from the dream usually reasonably accurate? Is the dream easily remembered?

RA: I am Ra. You must realize that we are overgeneralizing in order to answer your queries, as there are several sorts of dreams. However, in general, it may be noted that it is only for a trained and disciplined observer to have reasonably good recall of the dreaming. This faculty may be learned by virtue of a discipline of the recording immediately upon awakening of each and every detail which can be recalled. This training sharpens one's ability to recall the dream. The most common perception of a mind/body/spirit complex of dreams is muddied, muddled, and quickly lost.

QUESTIONER: In remembering dreams, then, you are saying that the individual can find specific clues to current energy center blockages and may, thereby, reduce or eliminate those blockages. Is this correct?

RA: I am Ra. This is so.

QUESTIONER: Is there any other function of dreaming that is of value in the evolutionary process?

RA: I am Ra. Although there are many which are of some value, we would choose two to note, since these two, though not of value in polarization, may be of value in a more generalized sense.

The activity of dreaming is an activity in which there is made a finely wrought and excellently fashioned bridge from conscious to unconscious. In this state the various distortions which have occurred in the energy web of the body complex, due to the misprision with which energy influxes have been received, are healed. With the proper amount of dreaming comes the healing of these distortions. Continued lack of this possibility can cause seriously distorted mind/body/ spirit complexes.

The other function of the dreaming which is of aid is that type of dream which is visionary and which prophets and mystics have experienced from days of old. Their visions come through the roots of mind and speak to a hungry world. Thus the dream is of service without being of a personally polarizing nature. However, in that mystic or prophet who desires to serve, such service will increase the entity's polarity.

QUESTIONER: There is a portion of sleep that has been called REM. Is this the state of dreaming?

RA: I am Ra. This is correct.

QUESTIONER: It was noticed that this occurs in small units during the night, with gaps in between. Is there any particular reason for this?

RA: I am Ra. Yes.

QUESTIONER: If it is of any value to know that, would you tell me why the dreaming process works like that?

RA: I am Ra. The portions of the dreaming process which are helpful for polarization and also for the vision of the mystic take place in time/space and, consequently, use the bridge from metaphysical to physical for what seems to be a brief period of your space/time. The time/space equivalent is far greater. The bridge remains, however, and traduces each distortion of mind, body, and spirit as it has received the distortions of energy influxes so that healing may take place. This healing process does not occur with the incidence of rapid eye movement but rather occurs largely in the space/time portion of the mind/ body/spirit complex using the bridge to time/space for the process of healing to be enabled.

QUESTIONER: You mentioned the loss of knowledge and control over the body as being a factor that was helpful in the evolutionary process due to veiling. Could you enumerate the important losses of knowledge and control of the body?

RA: I am Ra. This query contains some portions which would be more helpfully answered were some intervening material requested.

QUESTIONER: I'm at a loss to know what to request. Can you give me an idea of what area of intervening material I should work on?

RA: I am Ra. No. However, we shall be happy to answer the original query if it is still desired, if you first perceive that there is information lacking.

QUESTIONER: Perhaps I can question slightly differently here. I might ask why the loss of knowledge and control over the body was helpful?

RA: I am Ra. The knowledge of the potentials of the physical vehicle before the veiling offered the mind/body/spirit a free range of choices with regard to activities and manifestations of the body but offered little in the way of the development of polarity. When the knowledge of these potentials and functions of the physical vehicle is shrouded from the conscious-mind complex, the mind/body/spirit complex is often nearly without knowledge of how to best manifest its beingness. However, this state of lack of knowledge offers an opportunity for a desire to grow within the mind complex. This desire is that which seeks to know the possibilities of the body complex. The ramifications of each possibility and the eventual biases thusly built have within them a force which can only be generated by such a desire or will to know.

QUESTIONER: Perhaps you could give examples of the use of the body prior to veiling and after the veiling in the same aspect, to help us understand the change in knowledge of and control over the body more clearly. Could you do this, please?

RA: I am Ra. We could.

QUESTIONER: Will you do this?

RA: I am Ra. Yes. Let us deal with the sexual energy transfer. Before the veiling, such a transfer was always possible due to there being no shadow upon the grasp of the nature of the body and its relationship to other mind/body/spirits in this particular manifestation. Before the veiling process there was a near-total lack of the use of this sexual energy transfer beyond green ray.

This also was due to the same unshadowed knowledge each had

of each. There was, in third density then, little purpose to be seen in the more intensive relationships of mind, body, and spirit which you may call those of the mating process, since each other-self was seen to be the Creator and no other-self seemed to be more the Creator than another.

After the veiling process it became infinitely more difficult to achieve green-ray energy transfer due to the great areas of mystery and unknowing concerning the body complex and its manifestations. However, also due to the great shadowing of the manifestations of the body from the conscious-mind complex, when such energy transfer was experienced it was likelier to provide catalyst which caused a bonding of self with other-self in a properly polarized configuration.

From this point it was far more likely that higher energy transfers would be sought by this mated pair of mind/body/spirit complexes, thus allowing the Creator to know Itself with great beauty, solemnity, and wonder. Intelligent infinity having been reached by this sacramental use of this function of the body, each mind/body/spirit complex of the mated pair gained greatly in polarization and in ability to serve.

QUESTIONER: Did any of the other aspects of loss of knowledge or control of the body approach, to any degree in efficiency, the description which you have just given?

RA: I am Ra. Each function of the body complex has some potential after the veiling to provide helpful catalyst. We did choose the example of sexual energy transfer due to its central place in the functionary capabilities of the body complex made more useful by means of the veiling process.

This instrument grows somewhat low in energy. We would prefer to retain the maximal portion of reserved energy for which this instrument has given permission. We would, therefore, ask for one more full query at this working.

QUESTIONER: I would assume that the veiling of the sexual aspect was of great efficiency because it is an aspect that has to do totally with a relationship with an other-self. It would seem to me that the bodily veilings having to do with other-self interaction would be more efficient when compared with those only related to self, which would be lower in efficiency in producing either positive or negative polarization. Am I correct in this assumption?

RA: I am Ra. You are correct to a great extent. Perhaps the most notable exception is the attitude of one already strongly polarized negatively towards the appearance of the body complex. There are those entities upon the negative path which take great care in the preservation of the distortion your peoples perceive as fairness/ugliness. This fairness of form is, of course, then used in order to manipulate other-selves. May we ask if there are any brief queries?

QUESTIONER: Is there anything that we can do to make the instrument more comfortable or to improve the contact?

RA: I am Ra. We are pleased that this instrument was more conscientious in preparing itself for contact by means of the careful mental vibrations which you call prayer. This enabled the channel to be free from the distortions which the contact fell prey to during the last working.

We would suggest to the support group some continued care in the regulating of the physical activities of the instrument. However, at this nexus it is well to encourage those activities which feed the vital energies, as this instrument lives in this space/time present almost completely due to the careful adherence to the preservation of those mental and spiritual energies which make up the vital energy complex of this entity. Each is conscientious. The alignments are good.

We would caution the support group as to the physical alignment of the appurtenance known as the censer. There has been some slight difficulty due to variation in the pattern of the effluvium of this incense.

I am Ra. I leave you rejoicing in the power and in the peace of the One Infinite Creator. Go forth, then, rejoicing in the love and in the light of the One Creator. Adonai.

Session 87,
May 12, 1982

RA: I am Ra. I greet you in the love and in the light of the One Infinite Creator. I communicate now.

QUESTIONER: Could you first please give me the condition of the instrument?

RA: I am Ra. The distortions of the physical complex are unchanged. The vital energy levels are greatly enhanced.

QUESTIONER: Thank you. In considering what was mentioned in the last session about the censer, I have thought about the fact that the position of the origin of the smoke changes approximately 6 inches horizontally. Would it be better to have a censer in a single, horizontal smoking position?

RA: I am Ra. This alteration would be an helpful one, given that the censer is virgin.

QUESTIONER: What would be the optimum geometrical arrangement of censer, chalice, and candle with respect to the Bible and table and the positions that we now have them in?

RA: I am Ra. Both chalice and candle occupy the optimal configuration with respect to the book most closely aligned with the Law of One in the distortion complexes of this instrument. It is optimal to have the censer to the rear of this book and centered at the spine of its open configuration.

QUESTIONER: Would a position directly between the chalice and the candle be optimum, then, for the censer?

RA: I am Ra. This is not an exact measurement, since both chalice and candle are irregularly shaped. However, speaking roughly, this is correct.

QUESTIONER: Thank you. What is the present situation with respect to our fifth-density negative companion?

RA: I am Ra. This entity has withdrawn for a period of restoration of its polarity.

QUESTIONER: Would you expand upon the concept of the acquisition of polarity by this particular entity; its use, specifically, of this polarity other than the simple, obvious need for sixth-density harvest, if this is possible, please?

RA: I am Ra. We would. The nature of the densities above your own is that a purpose may be said to be shared by both positive and negative polarities. This purpose is the acquisition of the ability to welcome more and more the less and less distorted love/light and light/love of the One Infinite Creator. Upon the negative path, the wisdom density is one in which power over others has been refined until it is approaching absolute power. Any force such as the force your group and those of Ra offer which cannot be controlled by the power of such a negative fifth-density mind/body/spirit complex then depolarizes the entity which has not controlled other-self.

It is not within your conscious selves to stand against such refined power, but rather it has been through the harmony, the mutual love, and the honest calling for aid from the forces of light which have given you the shield and buckler.

QUESTIONER: What is the environmental situation of this particular fifth-density entity, and how does he work with fourth-density negative entities in order to establish power and control; what is his particular philosophy with respect to himself as Creator and with respect to the use of the first distortion and the extension of the first distortion to the fourth-density negative? I hope that this isn't too complex a question.

RA: I am Ra. The environment of your companion is that of the rock, the cave, the place of barrenness, for this is the density of wisdom, and that which is needed may be thought and received. To this entity, very little is necessary upon the physical, if you will, or space/time complex of distortions.

Such an entity spends its consciousness within the realms of time/space in an attempt to learn the ways of wisdom through the utmost use of the powers and resources of the self. Since the self is the Creator, the wisdom density provides many informative and fascinating experiences for the negatively polarized entity. In some respects, one may see a more lucid early attachment to wisdom from those of negative polarity, as the nexus of positions of consciousness upon which wisdom is laid is simpler.

The relationship of such an entity to fourth-density negative entities is one of the more powerful and the less powerful. The negative path posits slavery of the less powerful as a means of learning the desire to serve the self to the extent that the will is brought to bear. It is in this way that polarity is increased in the negative sense. Thus, fourth-density entities are willing slaves of such a fifth-density entity, there being no doubt whatsoever of the relative power of each.

QUESTIONER: A reflection of this could be seen in our density in many of those leaders who instigate war and have followers who support, in total conviction that the direction of conquest is correct. Is this correct?

RA: I am Ra. Any organization which demands obedience without question upon the basis of relative power is functioning according to the above-described plan.

QUESTIONER: One point that I am not clear on is the understanding and use of the first distortion by fifth- and fourth-density negative entities in manipulating third-density entities. I would like to know how the first distortion affects the attempts to carry out the conquest of third-density entities and the attempt to add them, under the premise of the first distortion, to their social memory complexes. Would you expand on that concept, please?

RA: I am Ra. This latter plan is not one of which fourth-density negative social memory complexes are capable. The fourth-density habit is that of offering temptations and of energizing preexisting distortions. Fourth-density entities lack the subtlety and magical practice which the fifth-density experience offers.

QUESTIONER: It seems, though, that in the case of many UFO contacts that have occurred on this planet that there must be some knowledge of and use of the first distortion. The fourth-density entities have carefully remained aloof and anonymous, you might say, for the most part, so that no proof in a concrete way of their existence is available. How are they oriented with respect to this type of contact?

RA: I am Ra. We misperceived your query, thinking it was directed towards this particular type of contact. The nature of the fourth density's observance of the free-will distortion, while pursuing the seeding of the third-density thought patterns, is material which has already been covered. That which can be offered of the negatively oriented information is offered. It is altered to the extent that the entity receiving such negative information is of positive orientation. Thus many such contacts are of a mixed nature.

QUESTIONER: I'm sorry for getting confused on my question here in not asking it correctly. There is a philosophical point of central importance that I am trying to clear up here. It has to do with the fact that fourth-density negative seems to be aware of the first distortion. They are in a nonveiled condition, and they seem to use this knowledge of the first distortion to maintain the situation that they maintain in contacts with this planet. I am trying to extract their ability to understand the mechanism of the first distortion and the consequences of the veiling process and still remain in a mental configuration of separation on the negative path. I hope that I have made myself clear there. I have had a hard time asking this question.

RA: I am Ra. The answer may still not satisfy the questioner. We ask that you pursue it until you are satisfied. The fourth-density negative entity has made the choice available to each at third-density harvest. It is aware of the full array of possible methods of viewing the universe of the One Creator, and it is convinced that the ignoring and nonuse of the green-ray energy center will be the method most efficient in providing harvestability of fourth density. Its operations among those of third density which have not yet made this choice are designed to offer to each the opportunity to consider the self-serving polarity and its possible attractiveness.

QUESTIONER: It seems to me that this is a service-to-others action in offering the possibility of the self-serving path. What is the relative effect of polarization in this action? I don't understand that.

RA: I am Ra. In your armed bands, a large group marauds and pillages successfully. The success of the privates is claimed by the corporals, the success of corporals by sergeants, then lieutenants, captains, majors, and finally the commanding general. Each successful temptation, each successful harvestable entity, is a strengthener of the power and polarity of the fourth-density social memory complex which has had this success.

QUESTIONER: If one mind/body/spirit complex is harvested from third density to a fourth-density social memory complex, is the total power of the social memory complex before the absorption of this single entity doubled when this entity is absorbed?

RA: I am Ra. No.

QUESTIONER: The Law of Doubling, then, does not work in this way. How much does the power of the social memory complex increase relative to this single entity that is harvested and absorbed into it?

RA: I am Ra. If one entity in the social memory complex is responsible for this addition to its being, that mind/body/spirit complex will absorb, in linear fashion, the power contained in the, shall we say, recruit. If a subgroup is responsible, the power is then this subgroup's. Only very rarely is the social memory complex of negative polarity capable of acting totally as one being. The loss of polarity due to this difficulty, to which we have previously referred as of kind of spiritual entropy, is quite large.

QUESTIONER: Then assuming that a single negatively oriented entity is responsible for the recruiting of a harvested third-density entity and adds its polarity to his negative polarity and power, what type of ability or what type of benefit is this, and how is it used by the entity?

RA: I am Ra. The so-called pecking order is immediately challenged, and the entity with increased power exercises that power to control more other-selves and to advance within the social memory complex structure.

QUESTIONER: How is this power measured? How is it obvious that this entity has gained this additional power?

RA: I am Ra. In some cases there is a kind of battle. This is a battle of wills, and the weapons consist of the light that can be formed by each contender. In most cases where the shift of power has been obvious, it simply is acknowledged, and those seeing benefit from associating with this newly more powerful entity aid it in rising within the structure.

QUESTIONER: Thank you. We noticed a possibility of confusion between the term "mind/body/spirit" and "mind/body/spirit complex" in the last session. Were there a couple of misuses of those terms in shifting one for the other?

RA: I am Ra. There was an error in transmission. The use of the term "mind/body/spirit" should refer to those entities dwelling in third density prior to the veiling process, the term "mind/body/spirit complex" referring to those entities dwelling in third density after the veiling process. We also discover a failure on our part to supply the term "complex" when speaking of body after the veiling. Please correct these errors. Also, we ask that you keep a vigilant watch over these transmissions for any errors, and question without fail, as it is our intention to provide as undistorted a series of sound vibration complexes as is possible.

This entity, though far better cleared of distortions towards the pain flares when prepared by those mental-vibration complexes you call prayer, is still liable to fluctuation due to its pre-incarnative body complex distortions and the energizing of them by those of negative polarity.

QUESTIONER: Thank you. We will make the corrections.[6] In the last session you made the statement that before the veiling, sexual energy transfer was always possible. I would like to know what you meant by "it was always possible" and why it was not always possible after the veiling, just to clear up that point?

RA: I am Ra. We believe that we grasp your query and will use the analogy in your culture of the battery which lights the flashlight bulb. Two working batteries placed in series always offer the potential of the bulb's illumination. After the veiling, to continue this gross analogy, the two batteries being placed not in series would then offer no possible illumination of the bulb. Many mind/body/spirit complexes after the veiling have, through blockages, done the equivalent of reversing the battery.

QUESTIONER: What was the primary source of the blockages that caused the battery reversal?

RA: I am Ra. Please query more specifically as to the mind/body/spirits or mind/body/spirit complexes about which you request information.

QUESTIONER: Before the veil, there was knowledge of the bulb-lighting technique, shall we say. After the veil, some experiments created a bulb lighting; some resulted in no bulb lighting. Other than the fact that information was not available on methods of lighting the bulb, was there some root cause of the experiments that resulted in no bulb lighting?
RA: I am Ra. This is correct.

QUESTIONER: What was this root cause?

RA: I am Ra. The root cause of blockage is the lack of the ability to see the other-self as the Creator, or, to phrase this differently, the lack of love.

QUESTIONER: In our particular illusion the sexual potential for the male seems to peak somewhere prior to the age twenty, and the female's peak is some ten years later. What is the cause of this difference in peaking sexual energy?

---

6. The text was corrected before printing and now reads as it should.

RA: I am Ra. We must make clear distinction between the yellow-ray, third-density, chemical bodily complex and the body complex which is a portion of the mind/body/spirit complex. The male, as you call this polarity, has an extremely active yellow-ray desire at the space/time in its incarnation when its sperm is the most viable and full of the life-giving spermato. Thusly the red ray seeks to reproduce most thickly at the time when this body is most able to fulfill the red-ray requirements.

The yellow-ray, chemical body complex of the female, as you call this polarity, must needs have a continued and increasing desire for the sexual intercourse, for it can only conceive once in one fifteen-to-eighteen-month period, given that it carries the conceived body complex, bears it, and suckles it. This is draining to the physical body of yellow ray. To compensate for this, the desire increases so that the yellow-ray body is predisposed to continue in sexual congress, thus fulfilling its red-ray requirement to reproduce as thickly as possible.

The more, shall we say, integral sexuality or polarity of the body complex, which is a portion of the mind/body/spirit complex, does not concern itself with these yellow-ray manifestations but rather follows the ways of the seeking of energy transfer and the furthering of aid and service to others or to the self.

QUESTIONER: In addition, why is the ratio of male to female orgasms so heavily loaded on the side of the male?

RA: I am Ra. We refer now to the yellow-ray physical body or, if you will, body complex. At this level the distinction is unimportant. The male orgasm, which motivates the sperm forward to meet its ovum, is essential for the completion of the red-ray desire to propagate the species. The female orgasm is unnecessary. Again, as mind/body/spirit complexes begin to use the sexual energy transfer to learn, to serve, and to glorify the One Infinite Creator, the function of the female orgasm becomes more clear.

QUESTIONER: What was this ratio before the veil?

RA: I am Ra. The ratio of male to female orgasms before the veil was closer to one to one by a great deal, as the metaphysical value of the female orgasm was clear and without shadow.

QUESTIONER: Is it meaningful to give this ratio in early fourth density, and, if so, would you do that?

RA: I am Ra. In many ways it is quite meaningless to speak of orgasm of male and female in higher densities, as the character and nature of orgasm becomes more and more naturally a function of the mind/body/ spirit complex as an unit. It may be said that the veil in fourth density is lifted and the choice has been made. In positive polarities, true sharing is almost universal. In negative polarities, true blockage so that the conqueror obtains orgasm, the conquered almost never is almost universal. In each case you may see the function of the sexual portion of experience as being a most efficient means of polarization.

QUESTIONER: In our illusion we have physical definitions for possible transfers of energy. We label them as the conversion of potential to kinetic or kinetic to heat and examine this with respect to the increasing entropy. When we speak of sexual energy transfers and other more basic forms of energy, I am always at a loss to properly use, you might say, the terms since I am not understanding—and possibly can't understand—the basic form of energy that we speak of. However, I intuit that this is the energy of pure vibration; that is, at the basic level of our illusion, that vibration between the space and time portion of the space/time continuum and yet somehow is transferred into our illusion in a more basic form than that. Could you expand on this area for me, please?

RA: I am Ra. Yes.

QUESTIONER: Would you do that?

RA: I am Ra. You are correct in assuming that the energy of which we speak in discussing sexual energy transfers is a form of vibratory bridge between space/time and time/space. Although this distinction is not apart from that which follows, that which follows may shed light upon that basic statement.

Due to the veiling process, the energy transferred from male to female is different than that transferred from female to male. Due to the polarity difference of the mind/body/spirit complexes of male and female, the male stores physical energy, the female mental and mental/ emotional energy. When third-density sexual energy transfer is completed, the male will have offered the discharge of physical energy. The female is, thereby, refreshed, having far less physical vitality. At the same time, if you will use this term, the female discharges the efflux of its stored mental and mental/emotional energy, thereby offering inspiration, healing, and blessing to the male, which by nature is less vital in this area.

At this time, may we ask for one more full query.

QUESTIONER: Why is the male and the female nature different?

RA: I am Ra. When the veiling process was accomplished, to the male polarity was attracted the Matrix of the Mind, and to the female, the Potentiator of the Mind; to the male, the Potentiator of the Body, to the female, the Matrix of the Body. May we ask if there are any brief queries before we close this working?

QUESTIONER: Is there anything that we can do to make the instrument more comfortable or to improve the contact?

RA: I am Ra. We shall find the suggested readjustment of the censer helpful. The alignments are good. You have been conscientious, my friends. We leave you now in the love and in the light of the One Infinite Creator. Go forth, therefore, rejoicing merrily in the power and in the ineffable peace of the One Infinite Creator. Adonai.

Session 88,
May 29, 1982

RA: I am Ra. I greet you in the love and in the light of the One Infinite Creator. We communicate now.

QUESTIONER: Could you first please give me the condition of the instrument?

RA: I am Ra. The physical-complex energy deficit is considerable at this space/time. There has been also a significant loss of the vital energies. However, these energies are still well within the distortion you may call strength.

QUESTIONER: Of all of the things that you have mentioned before for replenishing these energies, at this particular space/time, which would be most appropriate for the replenishing of both of these energies?

RA: I am Ra. As you note, there are many factors which contribute to the aiding of the strength distortions and the amelioration of distortions towards weakness in this instrument. We suggest to each that those many things which have been learned be conscientiously applied.

We would single out one physical distortion for discussion. The fourth-density negative minions which visit your group at this time are energizing a somewhat severe complex of imbalances in the manual appendages of this instrument and, to a lesser extent, those distortions of the thoracic region. We suggest care be taken to refrain from any unnecessary use of these appendages. As this instrument will not appreciate this suggestion, we suggest the appropriate discussion.

QUESTIONER: I assume from this that our fifth-density negative companion is still on R and R. Is this correct?

RA: I am Ra. Your fifth-density companion is not accompanying you at this time. However, it is not resting.

QUESTIONER: Is the censer that we have provided all right? It does go out prior to the end of the session. Would it be better if it did not go out prior to the end of the session?

RA: I am Ra. The new configuration of the censer is quite helpful to the more subtle patterns of energy surrounding these workings. It would be helpful to have a continuously burning amount of cense. However, the difficulty is in providing this without overpowering this enclosure with the amount of effluvium and physical product of combustion. Having to choose betwixt allowing the censer to finish its burning and having an overabundance of the smoke, we would suggest the former as being more helpful.

QUESTIONER: The instrument has mentioned what she refers to as bleed-through or being aware, during these sessions sometimes, of the communication. Would you comment on this?

RA: I am Ra. We have the mind/body/spirit complex of the instrument with us. As this entity begins to awaken from the metaphorical crib of experiencing light and activity in our density, it is beginning to be aware of the movement of thought. It does not grasp these thoughts any more than your third-density infant may grasp the first words it perceives. The experience should be expected to continue and is an appropriate outgrowth of the nature of these workings and of the method by which this instrument has made itself available to our words.

QUESTIONER: The instrument mentioned a recurrence of the need to go to the bathroom prior to the session. Is this because of the low vital energy?

RA: I am Ra. It is part of the cause of the lowered vital-energy level. This entity has been sustaining a level of the distortion you call pain which few among your peoples experience without significant draining of the energies. Indeed, the stability of the entity is notable. However, the entity has thusly become drained and further has felt other distortions such as those for a variety of experiences accentuated, for this is one means of balancing the inward-looking experience of the physical pain. Due to concern for this entity, such activities have been discouraged. This has further drained the entity.

The will to be of service to the Creator through the means of offering itself as instrument in these workings, therefore, was given an opportunity for the testing of resolve. This entity used some vital energy to fuel and replenish the will. No physical energy has been used by the instrument, but the vital energies were tapped so that this entity might have the opportunity to once again consciously choose to serve the One Infinite Creator.

QUESTIONER: Our publisher requests pictures for the book *The Law of One*, which is going to press at this time. Would you comment on the advisability, the benefit, or detriment, magical or otherwise, of us using pictures of this particular setup, the instrument, and the appurtenances in the book?

RA: I am Ra. The practical advisability of such a project is completely a product of your discrimination. There are magical considerations.

Firstly, if pictures be taken of a working the visual image must needs be that which is; that is, it is well for you to photograph only an actual working, and no sham nor substitution of any material. There shall be no distortions which this group can avoid any more than we would wish distortions in our words.

Secondly, it is inadvisable to photograph the instrument or any portion of the working room while the instrument is in trance. This is a narrow-band contact, and we wish to keep electrical and electromagnetic energies constant when their presence is necessary, and not present at all otherwise.

QUESTIONER: From what you . . . I'm sorry. Go ahead. If you meant to continue, continue. If not, I'll ask a question.

RA: I am Ra. We wished to state, thirdly, that once the instrumental is aware that the picture-taking will be performed, that during the entire picture-taking, whether before or after the working, the instrument be required to continuously respond to speech, thus assuring that no trance is imminent.

QUESTIONER: From what you have told me, then, I have planned the following: We will, after the session is complete and the instrument has been awakened, and before moving the instrument, have the instrument continually talk to us while I take pictures. In addition to this, I will take some other pictures as requested by the publisher. Is this the optimal filling of this requirement?

RA: I am Ra. Yes. We ask that any photographs tell the truth, that they be dated, and shine with a clarity so that there is no shadow of any but genuine expression which may be offered to those which seek truth. We come as humble messengers of the Law of One, desiring to decrease distortions. We ask that you, who have been our friends, work with any considerations such as above discussed, not with the thought of quickly removing an unimportant detail, but, as in all ways, regard such as another opportunity to, as the adept must, be yourselves and offer that which is in and with you without pretense of any kind.

QUESTIONER: Thank you. I would like to ask you as to the initial production of the Tarot—where this concept was first formed and where the Tarot was first recorded.

RA: I am Ra. The concept of the Tarot originated within the planetary influence you call Venus.

QUESTIONER: Was the concept given to or devised for a training tool for those inhabiting Venus at that time, or was it devised by those of Venus as a training tool for those of Earth?

RA: I am Ra. The Tarot was devised by the third-density population of Venus a great measure of your space/time in your past. As we have noted, the third-density experience of those of Venus dealt far more deeply and harmoniously with what you would call relationships with other-selves, sexual-energy-transfer work, and philosophical or metaphysical research. The product of many, many generations of work upon what we conceived to be the archetypical mind produced the Tarot which was used by our peoples as a training aid in developing the magical personality.

QUESTIONER: I'll make a guess that those of Venus of third density who were the initial ones to partially penetrate the veil gleaned information as to the nature of the archetypical mind and the veiling process and from this designed the Tarot as a method of teaching others. Is this correct?

RA: I am Ra. It is so.

QUESTIONER: I will also assume, and I may not be correct, that the present list that I have of twenty-two names of the Tarot cards of the Major Arcana are not in exact agreement with Ra's original generation of the Tarot. Could you describe the original Tarot, first telling me if there were twenty-two archetypes? That must have been the same. Were they the same as the list that I read to you in a previous session, or were there differences?

RA: I am Ra. As we have stated previously, each archetype is a concept complex and may be viewed not only by individuals but by those of the same racial and planetary influences in unique ways. Therefore, it is not informative to reconstruct the rather minor differences in descriptive terms between the Tarot used by us and that used by those of Egypt and the spiritual descendants of those first students of this system of study.

The one great breakthrough which was made after our work in third density was done was the proper emphasis given to the Arcanum Number Twenty-Two, which we have called The Choice. In our own experience we were aware that such an unifying archetype existed, but did not give that archetype the proper complex of concepts in order to most efficaciously use that archetype in order to promote our evolution.

QUESTIONER: I will make this statement as to my understanding of some of the archetypes and let you correct this statement. It seems to me that the Significators of Mind, Body, and Spirit are acted upon in each of these by the catalyst. This produces Experience, which then leads to the Transformation and produces the Great Way. This is the same process for the mind, the body, and spirit. The archetypes are just repeated but act in a different way as catalyst because of the differences of mind, body, and spirit and produce a different type of experience for each because of the difference in the three. The Transformation is slightly different. The Great Way is somewhat different, but the archetypes are all basically doing the same thing. They are just acting on three different portions of the mind/body/spirit complex so that we can say that in making the Significator a complex, basically we have provided a way for Catalyst to create the Transformation more efficiently. Would you correct that statement, please?

RA: I am Ra. In your statement, correctness is so plaited up with tendrils of the most fundamental misunderstanding that correction of your statement is difficult. We shall make comments and from these comments request that you allow a possible realignment of conceptualization to occur.

The archetypical mind is a great and fundamental portion of the mind complex, one of its most basic elements and one of the richest sources of information for the seeker of the One Infinite Creator. To attempt to condense the archetypes is to make an erroneous attempt. Each archetype is a significant *ding an sich,* or thing in itself, with its own complex of concepts. While it is informative to survey the relationships of one archetype to another, it can be said that this line of inquiry is secondary to the discovery of the purest gestalt or vision or melody which each archetype signifies to both the intellectual and intuitive mind.

The Significators of Mind, Body, and Spirit complexes are complex in and of themselves, and the archetypes of Catalyst, Experience, Transformation, and the Great Way are most fruitfully viewed as independent complexes which have their own melodies with which they may inform the mind of its nature.

We ask that you consider that the archetypical mind informs those thoughts which then may have bearing upon the mind, the body, or the spirit. The archetypes do not have a direct linkage to body or spirit. All must be drawn up through the higher levels of the subconscious mind to the conscious mind, and thence they may flee whither they have been bidden to go. When used in a controlled way they are most helpful. Rather than continue beyond the boundaries of your prior statement, we would appreciate the opportunity for your requestioning at this time so that we may answer you more precisely.

QUESTIONER: Did Ra use cards similar to the Tarot cards for training in third density?

RA: I am Ra. No.

QUESTIONER: What did Ra use in third density?

RA: I am Ra. You are aware in your attempts at magical visualization of the mental configuration of sometimes rather complex visualizations. These are mental and drawn with the mind. Another example well known in your culture is the visualization, in your mass, of the distortion of the love of the One Infinite Creator called Christianity, wherein a small portion of your foodstuffs is seen to be a mentally configured but entirely real man, the man known to you as Jehoshuah or, as you call this entity now, Jesus. It was by this method of sustained visualization over a period of training that we worked with these concepts.

These concepts were occasionally drawn. However, the concept of one visualization per card was not thought of by us.

QUESTIONER: How did the teacher relay information to the student in respect to visualization?

RA: I am Ra. The process was cabalistic; that is, of the oral tradition of mouth to ear.

QUESTIONER: Then when Ra attempted to teach the Egyptians the concept of the Tarot, was the same process used, or a different one?

RA: I am Ra. The same process was used. However, those which were teach/learners after us first drew these images to the best of their ability within the place of initiation and later began the use of what you call cards bearing these visualizations' representations.

QUESTIONER: Were the Court Arcana and the Minor Arcana a portion of Ra's teachings, or was this something that came along later?

RA: I am Ra. Those cards of which you speak were the product of the influence of those of Chaldea and Sumer.

QUESTIONER: You mentioned earlier that the Tarot was a method of divination. Would you explain that?

RA: I am Ra. We must first divorce the Tarot as a method of divination from this Major Arcana as representative of twenty-two archetypes of the archetypical mind.

The value of that which you call astrology is significant when used by those initiated entities which understand, if you will pardon the misnomer, the sometimes intricate considerations of the Law of Confusion. As each planetary influence enters the energy web of your sphere, those upon the sphere are moved much as the moon which moves about your sphere moves the waters upon your deeps. Your own nature is water, in that you as mind/body/spirit complexes are easily impressed and moved. Indeed, this is the very fiber and nature of your journey and vigil in this density: to not only be moved but to instruct yourself as to the preferred manner of your movement in mind, body, and spirit.

Therefore, as each entity enters the planetary energy web, each entity experiences two major planetary influxes, that of the conception, which has to do with the physical, yellow-ray manifestation of the incarnation, and that of the moment you call birth, when the breath is first drawn into the body complex of chemical yellow ray. Thus those who know the stars and their configurations and influences are able to see a rather broadly drawn map of the country through which an entity has traveled, is traveling, or may be expected to travel, be it upon the physical, the mental, or the spiritual level. Such an entity will have developed abilities of the initiate which are normally known among your peoples as psychic or paranormal.

When the archetypes are shuffled into the mix of astrologically oriented cards which form the so-called Court Arcana and Minor Arcana, these archetypes become magnetized to the psychic impressions of the one working with the cards, and thusly become instruments of a linkage between the practitioner of the astrological determinations and divinations and the one requesting information. Ofttimes, such archetypical representations will appear in such a manner as to have seemingly interesting results, meaningful in configuration to the questioner. In and of themselves, the Major Arcana have no rightful place in divination but, rather, are tools for the further knowledge of the self by the self for the purpose of entering a more profoundly, acutely realized present moment.

QUESTIONER: Ra must have had, shall we say, a lesson plan or course of training for the twenty-two archetypes to be given either to those of third density of Ra or, later on, to those in Egypt. Could you describe this scenario for the training course?

RA: I am Ra. This shall be the last full query of this working. We find it more nearly appropriate to discuss our plans in acquainting initiates upon your own planet with this particular version of the archetypes of the archetypical mind. Our first stage was the presentation of the images, one after the other, in the following order: one, eight, fifteen; two, nine, sixteen; three, ten, seventeen; four, eleven, eighteen; five, twelve, nineteen; six, thirteen, twenty; seven, fourteen, twenty-one; twenty-two. In this way the fundamental relationships between mind, body, and spirit could begin to be discovered, for as one sees, for instance, the Matrix of the Mind in comparison to the Matrices of Body and Spirit, one may draw certain tentative conclusions.

When, at length, the student had mastered these visualizations and had considered each of the seven classifications of archetype, looking at the relationships between mind, body, and spirit, we then suggested consideration of archetypes in pairs: one and two; three and four; five; six and seven. You may continue in this form for the body and spirit archetypes. You will note that the consideration of the Significator was left unpaired, for the Significator shall be paired with Archetype Twenty-Two.

At the end of this line of inquiry, the student was beginning to grasp more and more deeply the qualities and resonances of each archetype. At this point, using various other aids to spiritual evolution, we encouraged the initiate to learn to become each archetype and, most importantly, to know as best as possible within your illusion when the adoption of the archetype's persona would be spiritually or metaphysically helpful.

As you can see, much work was done creatively by each initiate. We have no dogma to offer. Each perceives that which is needful and helpful to the self.

May we ask if there are any brief queries before we leave this working?

QUESTIONER: Is there anything that we can do to improve the contact or to make the instrument more comfortable?

RA: I am Ra. We, again, ward you concerning the distortions of the instrument's hands. The fourth-density influence upon them could be inconvenient in that, if allowed to proceed without abatement, what you call your surgery shall be almost immediately necessary.

The alignments are good. You have been fastidious. We leave you, my friends, in the love and in the light of the One Infinite Creator. Go forth, therefore, rejoicing merrily in the power and in the glorious peace of the One Infinite Creator. Adonai.

Session 89,
June 9, 1982

RA: I am Ra. I greet you in the love and in the light of the One Infinite Creator. We communicate now.

QUESTIONER: Could you first please give me the condition of the instrument?

RA: I am Ra. It is as previously stated.

QUESTIONER: I have two questions, the first of which is: during the last intensive meditation here the instrument experienced very strong conditioning from an entity which did not identify itself and which did not leave when she asked it to. Would you tell us what was occurring then?

RA: I am Ra. We find the instrument to have been given the opportunity to become a channel for a previously known friend. This entity was not able to answer the questioning of spirits in the name of Christ as is this instrument's distortion of the means of differentiating betwixt those of positive and those of negative orientation. Therefore, after some resistance, the entity found the need to take its leave.

QUESTIONER: Was this particular entity the fifth-density visitor that we have had quite often previously?

RA: I am Ra. This is correct.

QUESTIONER: Is he back with us at this time?

RA: I am Ra. No. The attempt to speak was due to the vigilant eye of the minions of this entity, which noted what one may call a surge of natural telepathic ability upon the part of the instrument. This ability is cyclical, of the eighteen-diurnal-period cycle, as we have mentioned aforetimes. Thusly, this entity determined to attempt another means of access to the instrument by free will.

QUESTIONER: Was this what I would refer to as an increased ability to receive telepathically over a broader range of basic frequencies so as to include not only the Confederation but also this entity?

RA: I am Ra. This is incorrect. The high point of the cycle sharpens the ability to pick up the signal but does not change the basic nature of the carrier wave. Shall we say, there is greater power in the receiving antennae.

QUESTIONER: This question may be meaningless, but would a

fifth-density entity of the Confederation who was positively polarized transmit on the same frequency as our negatively polarized fifth-density companion?

RA: I am Ra. This is correct and is the reason that the questioning of all contacts is welcomed by the Confederation of Planets in the Service of the Infinite Creator.

QUESTIONER: Question 2: [Name] has also felt some conditioning which was unbidden while channeling Latwii recently and in his personal meditations. Could you also tell us what occurred in these cases?

RA: I am Ra. The entity which has been companion has a vibratory frequency but a small amount lesser than that of the social memory complex known as Latwii. Also, Latwii is the primary Comforter of the Confederation for entities seeking at the vibratory-complex level of the one known as [name]. Therefore, this same companion has been attempting the contact of this instrument also, although this instrument would have great difficulty in distinguishing the actual contact due to the lack of experience of your companion at this type of service. Nevertheless, it is well that this instrument also choose some manner of the challenging of contacts.

QUESTIONER: How many of our years ago was Ra's third density ended?

RA: I am Ra. The calculations necessary for establishing this point are difficult, since so much of what you call time is taken up before and after third density as you see the progress of time from your vantage point. We may say in general that the time of our enjoyment of the choice-making was approximately 2.6 million of your sun-years in your past. However—we correct this instrument. Your term is billion, 2.6 billion of your years in your past. However, this time, as you call it, is not meaningful, for our intervening space/time has been experienced in a manner quite unlike your third-density experience of space/time.

QUESTIONER: It appears that the end of Ra's third density coincided with the beginning of this planet's second density. Is that correct?

RA: I am Ra. This is roughly correct.

QUESTIONER: Did the planet Venus become a fourth-density planet at that time?

RA: I am Ra. This is so.

QUESTIONER: Did it later, then, become a fifth-density planet?

RA: I am Ra. It later became a fourth/fifth-density planet; then, later a fifth-density planet for a large measure of your time. Both fourth- and fifth-density experiences were possible upon the planetary influence of what you call Venus.

QUESTIONER: What is its density at present?

RA: I am Ra. Its core vibrational frequency is sixth density. However we, as a social memory complex, have elected to leave that influence. Therefore, the beings inhabiting this planetary influence at this space/time are fifth-density entities. The planet may be considered a fifth/sixth-density planet.

QUESTIONER: What was your reason for leaving?

RA: I am Ra. We wished to be of service.

QUESTIONER: I have here a deck of twenty-two Tarot cards which have been copied, according to information we have, from the walls of the large pyramid at Giza. If necessary we can duplicate these cards in the book which we are preparing. I would ask Ra if these cards represent an exact replica of that which is in the Great Pyramid.

RA: I am Ra. The resemblance is substantial.

QUESTIONER: In other words, you might say that these were better than 95 percent correct as far as representing what is on the walls of the Great Pyramid?

RA: I am Ra. Yes.

QUESTIONER: The way that I understand this, then, Ra gave these archetypical concepts to the priests of Egypt, who then drew them upon the walls of one of the chambers of the Great Pyramid. What was the technique of transmission of this information to the priests? At this time was Ra walking the surface among the Egyptians, or was this done through some form of channeling?

RA: I am Ra. This was done partially through old teachings and partially through visions.

QUESTIONER: Then at this particular time, Ra had long since vacated the planet as far as walking among the Egyptians. Is this correct?

RA: I am Ra. Yes.

QUESTIONER: I would like to question Ra on each of these cards, in order to better understand the archetypes. Is this agreeable?

RA: I am Ra. As we have previously stated, these archetypical-concept complexes are a tool for learn/teaching. Thusly, if we were to offer information that were not a response to observations of the student, we would be infringing upon the free will of the learn/teacher by being teach/learner and learn/teacher at once.

QUESTIONER: You stated that Ra used the Tarot to develop the magical personality. Was this done to mentally become the essence of each archetype and in this way develop the magical personality?

RA: I am Ra. This is incorrect. The clothing one's self within the archetype is an advanced practice of the adept which has long studied this archetypical system. The concept complexes which together are intended to represent the architecture of a significant and rich portion of the mind are intended to be studied as individual concept complexes as Matrix, Potentiator, etc. in viewing mind/body/spirit connections and in pairs with some concentration upon the polarity of the male and the female. If these are studied, there comes the moment when the deep threnodies and joyful ditties of the deep mind can successfully be brought forward to intensify, articulate, and heighten some aspect of the magical personality.

QUESTIONER: You stated that each archetype is a concept complex. Would you please define what you mean by that statement?

RA: I am Ra. Upon the face of it, such a definition is without merit, being circular. A concept complex is a complex of concepts just as a molecule is a complex structure made up of more than one type of energy nexus or atom. Each atom within a molecule is its unique identity and, by some means, can be removed from the molecule. The molecule of water can, by chemical means, be caused to separate into hydrogen and oxygen. Separately they cannot be construed to equal water. When formed in the molecular structure which exemplifies water, the two are irrefragably water.

Just in this way, each archetype has within it several root atoms of organizational being. Separately the overall structure of the complex cannot be seen. Together the concept complex is irrefragably one thing. However, just as it is most useful in grasping the potentials in your physical systems of the constituted nature of water, so in grasping the nature of an archetype it is useful to have a sense of its component concepts.

QUESTIONER: In Archetype One, represented by Tarot card number 1, the Matrix of the Mind seems to have four basic parts to the complex. Looking at the card, we have, first and most obvious, the Magician and what seems to be an approaching star. A stork or similar bird seems to be in a cage. On top of the cage seems to be something that seems to be very difficult to discern. Am I in any way correct in this analysis?

RA: I am Ra. You are competent at viewing pictures. You have not yet grasped the nature of the Matrix of the Mind as fully as is reliably possible upon contemplation. We would note that the representations drawn by priests were somewhat distorted by acquaintance with and dependence upon the astrologically based teachings of the Chaldees.

QUESTIONER: When Ra originally trained or taught the Egyptians about the Tarot, did Ra act as teach/learners to a degree that Ra became learn/teachers?

RA: I am Ra. This distortion we were spared.

QUESTIONER: Then could you tell me what information you gave to the Egyptian priests who first were contacted or taught with respect to the first archetype? Is this possible for you to do within the limits of the first distortion?

RA: I am Ra. It is possible. Our first step, as we have said, was to present the descriptions in verbal form of three images: one, eight, fifteen; then the questions were asked: "What do you feel that a bird might represent?" "What do you feel that a wand might represent?" "What do you feel that the male represents?" And so forth, until those studying were working upon a system whereby the images used became evocative of a system of concepts. This is slow work when done for the first time.

We may note, with sympathy, that you undoubtedly feel choked by the opposite difficulty, that of a great mass of observation upon this system, all of which has some merit, as each student will experience the archetypical mind and its structure in an unique way useful to that student. We suggest that one or more of this group do that which we have suggested, in order that we may, without infringement, offer observations on this interesting subject which may be of further aid to those inquiring in this area.

We would note at this time that the instrument is having almost continuous pain flares. Therefore, we ask that each of the support group be especially aware of any misinformation in order that we may correct any distortions of information the soonest possible.

QUESTIONER: Now as I understand it, what you suggest as far as the Tarot goes is to study the writings that we have available, and from those formulate questions. Is this correct?

RA: I am Ra. No.

QUESTIONER: I'm sorry that I didn't understand exactly what you meant with respect to this. Would it be appropriate then for me to answer the questions with what I think is the meaning of the three items that you spoke of for Card Number One and then Card Eight, etc.? Is this what you mean?

RA: I am Ra. This is very close to our meaning. It was our intention to suggest that one or more of you go through the plan of study which we have suggested. The queries having to do with the archetypes as found in the Tarot after this point may take the form of observing what seem to be the characteristics of each archetype, relationships between mind, body, and spiritual archetypes of the same ranking such as Matrix, or archetypes as seen in relationship to polarity, especially when observed in the pairings.

Any observations made by a student which have fulfilled the considerations will receive our comment in return. Our great avoidance of interpreting, for the first time, for the learn/teacher various elements of a picture upon a piece of pasteboard is involved both with the Law of Confusion and with the difficulties of the distortions of the pictures upon the pasteboard. Therefore, we may suggest a conscientious review of that which we have already given concerning this subject, as opposed to the major reliance being either upon any rendition of the archetype pictures or any system which has been arranged as a means of studying these pictures.

QUESTIONER: All right; I'll have to do that. Ra stated that a major breakthrough was made when proper emphasis was put on Arcanum Twenty-Two. This didn't happen until Ra had completed third density. I assume from this that Ra, being polarized positively, probably had some of the same difficulty that occurred prior to the veil, in that the negative polarity was not appreciated. That's a guess. Is this correct?

RA: I am Ra. In one way it is precisely correct. Our harvest was overwhelmingly positive, and our appreciation of those which were negative was relatively uninformed. However, we were intending to suggest that in the use of the system known to you as the Tarot, for advancing the spiritual evolution of the self, a proper understanding, if we may use this misnomer, of Archetype Twenty-Two is greatly helpful in sharpening the basic view of the Significator of Mind, Body, and Spirit and, further, throws into starker relief the Transformation and Great Way of Mind, Body, and Spirit complexes.

QUESTIONER: Were some of Ra's population negatively harvested at the end of Ra's third density?

RA: I am Ra. We had no negative harvest as such, although there had been two entities which had harvested themselves during the third density in the negative or service-to-self path. There were, however, those upon the planetary surface during third density whose vibratory patterns were in the negative range but were not harvestable.

QUESTIONER: What was Ra's average total population incarnate on Venus in third density?

RA: I am Ra. We were a small population which dwelt upon what you would consider difficult conditions. Our harvest was approximately six million five hundred thousand mind/body/spirit complexes. There were approximately thirty-two million mind/body/spirit complexes repeating third density elsewhere.

QUESTIONER: What was the attitude prior to harvest of those harvestable entities of Ra with respect to those who were obviously unharvestable?

RA: I am Ra. Those of us which had the gift of polarity felt deep compassion for those who seemed to dwell in darkness. This description is most apt, as ours was a harshly bright planet in the physical sense.

There was every attempt made to reach out with whatever seemed to be needed. However, those upon the positive path have the comfort of companions, and we of Ra spent a great deal of our attention upon the possibilities of achieving spiritual or metaphysical adepthood or work in indigo ray through the means of relationships with other-selves. Consequently, the compassion for those in darkness was balanced by the appreciation of the light.

QUESTIONER: Would Ra have the same attitude toward the unharvestable entities or would it be different at this nexus than at the time of harvest from the third density?

RA: I am Ra. Not substantially. To those who wish to sleep, we could only offer those comforts designed for the sleeping. Service is only possible to the extent it is requested. We were ready to serve in whatever way we could. This still seems satisfactory as a means of dealing with other-selves in third density. It is our feeling that to be each entity which one attempts to serve is to simplify the grasp of what service is necessary or possible.

QUESTIONER: What techniques did the two negatively harvested entities use for negative polarization upon such a positively polarized planet?

RA: I am Ra. The technique of control over others and domination unto the physical death was used in both cases. Upon a planetary influence much unused to slaughter, these entities were able to polarize by this means. Upon your third-density environment at the time of your experiencing, such entities would merely be considered, shall we say, ruthless despots which waged the holy war.

QUESTIONER: Did these two entities evolve from the second density of the planet Venus along with the rest of the population of Venus that became Ra from second density to third?

RA: I am Ra. No.

QUESTIONER: What was the origin of the two entities of which you speak?

RA: I am Ra. These entities were Wanderers from early positive fifth density.

QUESTIONER: And though they had already evolved through a positive fourth density, they, shall we say, switched polarity in the reincarnating in third density. Is this correct?

RA: I am Ra. This is correct.

QUESTIONER: What was the catalyst for their change?

RA: I am Ra. In our peoples there was what may be considered, from the viewpoint of wisdom, an overabundance of love. These entities looked at those still in darkness and saw that those of a neutral or somewhat negative viewpoint found such harmony, shall we say, sickening. The Wanderers felt that a more wisdom-oriented way of seeking love could be more appealing to those in darkness.

First one entity began its work. Quickly the second found the first. These entities had agreed to serve together and so they did, glorifying the One Creator, but not as they intended. About them were soon gathered those who found it easy to believe that a series of specific knowledges and wisdoms would advance one towards the Creator. The end of this was the graduation into fourth-density negative of the Wanderers, which had much power of personality, and some small deepening of the negatively polarized element of those not polarizing positively. There was no negative harvest as such.

QUESTIONER: What was the reason for the wandering of these two Wanderers, and were they male and female?

RA: I am Ra. All Wanderers come to be of assistance in serving the Creator, each in its own way. The Wanderers of which we have been speaking were indeed incarnated male and female, as this is by far the most efficient system of partnership.

QUESTIONER: As a wild guess, one of these entities wouldn't be the one who has been our companion here for some time, would it?

RA: I am Ra. No.

QUESTIONER: Then from what you say, I am guessing that these Wanderers returned or wandered to Ra's third density possibly to seed greater wisdom in what they saw as an overabundance of compassion in the Ra culture. Is this correct?

RA: I am Ra. This is incorrect in the sense that before incarnation, it was the desire of these Wanderers only to aid in service to others. The query has correctness when seen from the viewpoint of the Wanderers within that incarnation.

QUESTIONER: I just can't understand why they would think that a planet that was doing as well as the population of Venus was doing, as far as I can tell, would need Wanderers in order to help with the harvest. Was this at an early point in Ra's third density?

RA: I am Ra. It was in the second cycle of 25,000 years. We had a harvest of six out of thirty, to speak roughly, of millions of mind/body/spirit complexes, less than 20 percent. Wanderers are always drawn to whatever percentage has not yet polarized, and come when there is a call. There was a call from those which were not positively polarized as such but which sought to be positively polarized and sought wisdom, feeling the compassion of other-selves upon Venus as complacent or pitying towards other-selves.

QUESTIONER: What was the attitude of these two entities after they graduated into fourth-density negative and, the veil being removed, realized that they had switched polarities?

RA: I am Ra. They were disconcerted.

QUESTIONER: Then did they continue striving to polarize negatively for a fifth-density harvest in the negative sense, or did they do something else?

RA: I am Ra. They worked with the fourth-density negative for some period until, within this framework, the previously learned patterns of the self had been recaptured and the polarity was, with great effort, reversed. There was a great deal of fourth-density positive work then to be retraced.

QUESTIONER: How is Ra aware of this information? By what means does Ra know the precise orientation of these two entities in fourth-density negative, etc.?

RA: I am Ra. These entities joined Ra in fourth-density positive for a portion of the cycle which we experienced.

QUESTIONER: I assume, then, that they came in late. Is this correct?

RA: I am Ra. Yes.

QUESTIONER: I didn't mean to get so far off the track of my original direction, but I think that some of these excursions are enlightening and will help in understanding the basic mechanisms that we are so interested in, in evolution.

Ra stated that archetypes are helpful when used in a controlled way. Would you give me an example of what you mean by using an archetype in a controlled way?

RA: I am Ra. We speak with some regret in stating that this shall be our last query of length. There is substantial energy left, but this instrument has distortions that rapidly approach the limit of our ability to maintain secure contact.

The controlled use of the archetypes is that which is done within the self for the polarization of the self and to the benefit of the self, if negatively polarized, or others, if positively polarized, upon the most subtle of levels.

Keep in mind at all times that the archetypical mind is a portion of the deep mind and informs thought processes. When the archetype is translated without regard for magical propriety into the manifested daily actions of an individual, the greatest distortions may take place, and great infringement upon the free will of others is possible. This is more nearly acceptable to one negatively polarized. However, the more carefully polarized of negative mind/body/spirit complexes will also prefer to work with a finely tuned instrument. May we ask if there are any brief queries before we leave this working?

QUESTIONER: I'll just make the statement that I perceive that a negative-polarity harvest is possible with less negativity in the environment like Ra's environment than in the environment such as we have at present, and ask if that is correct, and then is there anything that we can do to improve the contact or the comfort of the instrument?

RA: I am Ra. Firstly, the requirements of harvest are set. It is, however, easier to serve the self completely or nearly so if there is little resistance.

In the matter of the nurturing of the instrument, we suggest further manipulation of the dorsal side and appendages of this instrument and the whirling of the waters, if possible. The alignments are conscientious. We ask for your vigilance in alignments and preparations. All is well, my friends.

I am Ra. I leave you in the love and in the light of the One Infinite Creator. Go forth, then, rejoicing in the power and in the peace of the One Infinite Creator. Adonai.

Session 90,
June 19, 1982

RA: I am Ra. I greet you in the love and in the light of the One Infinite Creator. We communicate now.

QUESTIONER: Could you first please give me the condition of the instrument?

RA: I am Ra. The physical-complex energy deficit is somewhat increased by continued distortions towards pain. The vital energy levels are as previously stated, having fluctuated slightly between askings.

QUESTIONER: Could you tell me the situation with respect to our fourth- and fifth-density companions at this time?

RA: I am Ra. The fourth-density league of companions accompanies your group. The fifth-density friend, at this space/time nexus, works within its own density exclusively.

QUESTIONER: By what means do these particular fourth-density entities get from their origin to our position?

RA: I am Ra. The mechanism of calling has been previously explored. When a distortion which may be negatively connotated is effected, this calling occurs. In addition, the light of which we have spoken, emanating from attempts to be of service to others in a fairly clear and lucid sense, is another type of calling in that it represents that which requires balance by temptation. Thirdly, there have been certain avenues into the mind/body/spirit complexes of this group which have been made available by your fifth-density friend.

QUESTIONER: Actually, the question that I intended was, how do they get here? By what means of moving do they get here?

RA: I am Ra. In the mechanism of the calling, the movement is as you would expect; that is, the entities are within your planetary influence and are, having come through the quarantine web, free to answer such calling.

The temptations are offered by those negative entities of what you would call your inner planes. These, shall we say, dark angels have been impressed by the service-to-self path offered by those which have come through quarantine from days of old, and these entities, much like your angelic presences of the positive nature, are ready to move in thought within the inner planes of this planetary influence working from time/space to space/time.

The mechanism of the fifth-density entity is from density to density and is magical in nature. The fourth density, of itself, is not capable of building the highway into the energy web. However, it is capable of using that which has been left intact. These entities are, again, the Orion entities of fourth density.

QUESTIONER: You stated previously that fifth-density entities bear a resemblance to those of us in third density on planet Earth, but fourth density does not. Could you describe the fourth-density entities and tell me why they do not resemble us?

RA: I am Ra. The description must be bated under the Law of Confusion. The cause for a variety of so-called physical vehicles is the remaining variety of heritages from second-density physical vehicular forms. The process of what you call physical evolution continues to hold sway into fourth density. Only when the ways of wisdom have begun to refine the power of what you may loosely call thought is the form of the physical-complex manifestation more nearly under the direction of the consciousness.

QUESTIONER: If the population of this planet presently looks similar to fifth-density entities, I was wondering why this is. If I understand you correctly, the process of evolution would normally be that of third density resembling that from which evolved in second density and refining it in fourth and then again in fifth density, becoming what the population of this looks like in the third density. It seems to me that this planet is ahead of itself by the way that its mind/body/spirit complex or body complex looks. What is the reason for this?

RA: I am Ra. Your query is based upon a misconception. Do you wish us to comment or do you wish to requestion?

QUESTIONER: Please comment on my misconception, if that is possible.

RA: I am Ra. In fifth density the manifestation of the physical complex is more and more under the control of the conscious-mind complex. Therefore, the fifth-density entity may dissolve one manifestation and create another. Consequently, the choice of a fifth-density entity or complex of entities wishing to communicate with your peoples would be to resemble your peoples' physical-complex, chemical, yellow-ray vehicles.

QUESTIONER: I see. Very roughly, if you were to move a third-density entity from some other planet to this planet, what percentage of all of those within the knowledge of Ra would look enough like entities of Earth so that they would go unnoticed in a crowd?

RA: I am Ra. Perhaps 5 percent.

QUESTIONER: Then there is an extreme variation in the form of the physical vehicle in third density in the universe. I assume that this is also true of fourth density. Is this correct?

RA: I am Ra. This is so. We remind you that it is a great theoretical distance between demanding that the creatures of an infinite creation be unnoticeably similar to one's self, and observing those signs which may be called human which denote the third-density characteristics of self-consciousness, the grouping into pairs, societal groups, and races, and the further characteristic means of using self-consciousness to refine and search for the meaning of the milieu.

QUESTIONER: Within Ra's knowledge of the third-density physical forms, what percentage would be similar enough to this planet's physical forms that we would assume the entities to be human even though they were a bit different? This would have to be very rough because of my definition's being very rough.

RA: I am Ra. This percentage is still small; perhaps 13 to 15 percent due to the capabilities of various second-density life forms to carry out each necessary function for third-density work. Thusly to be observed would be behavior indicating self-consciousness and purposeful interaction with a sentient ambiance about the entity, rather than those characteristics which familiarly connote to your peoples the humanity of your third-density form.

QUESTIONER: Now, in this line of questioning, I am trying to link to the creations of various Logoi and their original use of a system of archetypes in their creation, and I apologize for a lack of efficiency in doing this, but I find this somewhat difficult. For this particular Logos in the beginning, prior to Its creation of the first density, did the archetypical system which it had chosen include the forms that would evolve in third density, or was this related to the archetypical concept at all?

RA: I am Ra. The choice of form is prior to the formation of the archetypical mind. As the Logos creates Its plan for evolution, then the chosen form is invested.

QUESTIONER: Was there a reason for choosing the forms that have evolved on this planet, and, if so, what was it?

RA: I am Ra. We are not entirely sure why our Logos and several neighboring Logoi of approximately the same space/time of flowering chose the bipedal, erect form of the second-density apes to invest. It has been our supposition, which we share with you as long as you are aware that this is mere opinion, that our Logos was interested in, shall we say, further intensifying the veiling process by offering to the third-density form the near-complete probability for the development of speech taking complete precedence over concept communication or telepathy. We also have the supposition that the so-called opposable thumb was looked upon as an excellent means of intensifying the veiling process, so that rather than rediscovering the powers of the mind, the third-density entity would, by the form of its physical manifestation, be drawn to the making, holding, and using of physical tools.

QUESTIONER: I will guess that the system of archetypes then was devised to further extend these particular principles. Is this correct?

RA: I am Ra. The phrasing is faulty. However, it is correct that the images of the archetypical mind are the children of the third-density physical manifestations of form of the Logos which has created the particular evolutionary opportunity.

QUESTIONER: Now, as I understand it, the archetypes are the biases of a very fundamental nature that, under free will, generate the experiences of each entity. Is this correct?

RA: I am Ra. The archetypical mind is part of that mind which informs all experience. Please recall the definition of the archetypical mind as the repository of those refinements to the cosmic or all-mind made by this particular Logos and peculiar only to this Logos. Thus it may be seen as one of the roots of mind, not the deepest but certainly the most informative in some ways. The other root of mind to be recalled is that racial or planetary mind which also informs the conceptualizations of each entity to some degree.

QUESTIONER: At what point in the evolutionary process does the archetypical mind first have effect upon the entity?

RA: I am Ra. At the point at which an entity, either by accident or design, reflects an archetype, the archetypical mind resonates. Thusly, random activation of the archetypical resonances begins almost immediately in third-density experience. The disciplined use of this tool of evolution comes far later in this process.

QUESTIONER: What was the ultimate objective of this Logos in designing the archetypical mind as It did?

RA: I am Ra. Each Logos desires to create a more eloquent expression of experience of the Creator by the Creator. The archetypical mind is intended to heighten this ability to express the Creator in patterns more like the fanned peacock's tail, each facet of the Creator vivid, upright, and shining with articulated beauty.

QUESTIONER: Is Ra familiar with the archetypical mind of some other Logos that is not the same as the one we experience?

RA: I am Ra. There are entities of Ra which have served as far Wanderers to those of another Logos. The experience has been one which staggers the intellectual and intuitive capacities, for each Logos sets up an experiment enough at variance from all others that the subtleties of the archetypical mind of another Logos are most murky to the resonating mind, body, and spirit complexes of this Logos.

QUESTIONER: There seems to have been created by this Logos, to me anyway, a large percentage of entities whose distortion was towards warfare. There have been the Maldek and Mars experiences and now Earth. It seems that Venus was the exception to what we could almost call the rule of warfare. Is this correct, and was this envisioned and planned into the construction of the archetypical mind, possibly not with respect to warfare as we have experienced it but as to the extreme action of polarization in consciousness?

RA: I am Ra. It is correct that the Logos designed Its experiment to attempt to achieve the greatest possible opportunities for polarization in third density. It is incorrect that warfare of the types specific to your experiences was planned by the Logos. This form of expression of hostility is an interesting result which is apparently concomitant with the tool-making ability. The choice of the Logos to use the life form with the grasping thumb is the decision to which this type of warfare may be traced.

QUESTIONER: Then did our Logos hope to see generated a positive and negative harvest from each density up to the sixth, starting with the third, as being the most efficient form of generating experience known to It at the time of Its construction of this system of evolution?

RA: I am Ra. Yes.

QUESTIONER: Then built into the basis for the archetypes is possibly the mechanism for creating the polarization in consciousness for service to others and service to self. Is this, in fact, true?

RA: I am Ra. Yes. You will notice the many inborn biases which hint to the possibility of one path's being more efficient than the other. This was the design of the Logos.

QUESTIONER: Then what you are saying is that once the path is recognized, either the positive or the negative polarized entity can find hints along his path as to the efficiency of that path. Is this correct?

RA: I am Ra. That which you say is correct upon its own merits but is not a repetition of our statement. Our suggestion was that within the experiential nexus of each entity within its second-density environment and within the roots of mind, there were placed biases indicating to the watchful eye the more efficient of the two paths. Let us say, for want of a more precise adjective, that this Logos has a bias towards kindness.

QUESTIONER: Then you say that the more efficient of the two paths was suggested in a subliminal way to second density to be the service-to-others path. Am I correct?

RA: I am Ra. We did not state which was the more efficient path. However, you are correct in your assumption, as you are aware from having examined each path in some detail in previous querying.

QUESTIONER: Could this be the reason for the greater positive harvest? I suspect that it isn't, but would there be Logoi that have greater negative-percentage harvests because of this type of biasing?

RA: I am Ra. No. There have been Logoi with greater percentages of negative harvests. However, the biasing mechanisms cannot change the requirements for achieving harvestability either in the positive or in the negative sense. There are Logoi which have offered a neutral background against which to polarize. This Logos chose not to do so but instead to allow more of the love and light of the Infinite Creator to be both inwardly and outwardly visible and available to the sensations and conceptualizations of mind/body/spirit complexes undergoing Its care in experimenting.

QUESTIONER: Were there any other circumstances, biases, consequences, or plans set up by the Logos other than those we have discussed for the evolution of Its parts through the densities?

RA: I am Ra. Yes.

QUESTIONER: What were these?

RA: I am Ra. One more; that is, the permeability of the densities so that there may be communication from density to density and from plane to plane or sub-density to sub-density.

QUESTIONER: Then as I see the plan for the evolution by this Logos, it was planned to create as vivid an experience as possible but also one which was somewhat informed with respect to the Infinite Creator and able to accelerate the progress as a function of will because of the permeability of densities. Have I covered accurately the general plan of this Logos with respect to Its evolution?

RA: I am Ra. Excepting the actions of the unmanifested self and the actions of self with other-self, you have been reasonably thorough.

QUESTIONER: Then, is the major mechanism forming the ways and very essence of the experience that we presently experience here the archetypical mind and the archetypes?

RA: I am Ra. These resources are a part of that which you refer to.

QUESTIONER: What I am really asking is what percentage of a part, roughly, are these responsible for?

RA: I am Ra. We ask once again that you consider that the archetypical mind is a part of the deep mind. There are several portions to this mind. The mind may serve as a resource. To call the archetypical mind the foundation of experience is to oversimplify the activities of the mind/body/spirit complex. To work with your query as to percentages is, therefore, enough misleading in any form of direct answer that we would ask that you requestion.

QUESTIONER: That's OK. I don't think that was too good a question anyway.

When Ra initially planned for helping the Egyptians with their evolution, what was the primary concept, and also secondary and tertiary if you can name those, that Ra wished to impart to the Egyptians? In other words, what was Ra's training plan or schedule for making the Egyptians aware of what was necessary for their evolution?

RA: I am Ra. We came to your peoples to enunciate the Law of One. We wished to impress upon those who wished to learn of unity that in unity, all paradoxes are resolved; all that is broken is healed; all that is forgotten is brought to light. We had no teaching plan, as you have called it, in that our intention when we walked among your peoples was to manifest that which was requested by those learn/teachers to which we had come.

We are aware that this particular line of querying—that is, the nature and architecture of the archetypical mind—has caused the questioner to attempt, to its own mind unsuccessfully, to determine the relative importance of these concepts. We cannot learn/teach for any, nor would we take this opportunity from the questioner. However, we shall comment.

The adept has already worked much, not only within the red, orange, yellow, and green energy centers but also in the opening of blue and indigo. Up through this point the archetypes function as the great base or plinth of a builded structure or statue, keeping the mind complex viable, level, and available as a resource whenever it may be evoked. There is a point at which the adept takes up its work. This is the point at which a clear and conscious consideration of the archetypical mind is useful.

QUESTIONER: I have an observation on Archetype Number One made by [name], and I request comment on it by Ra. I will read it: "The Matrix of the Mind is the conscious mind and is sustained by the power of the spirit as symbolized by the star which flows to it through the subconscious mind. It contains the will, which is signified by the scepter of power in the Magician's hand. All of creation is made through the power of the will directed by the conscious mind of the Magician, and the bird in the cage represents the illusion in which the self seems trapped. The Magician represents maleness or the radiance of being manifested as the creation through which each entity moves."

RA: I am Ra. As this instrument is becoming somewhat weary, we shall not begin this considerable discussion. We would request that this series of observations be repeated at the outset of the next working. We would suggest that each concept be discussed separately, or, if appropriate, a pair of concepts be related one to the other within the concept complex. This is slow work but shall make the eventual building of the concept complexes more smoothly accomplished.

Were we to have answered the observations as read by you at this space/time, as much space/time would have been given to the untangling of various concepts as to the building up of what were very thoughtful perceptions.

May we ask if there are any brief queries at this time?

QUESTIONER: Is there anything that we can do to make the instrument more comfortable or to improve the contact?

RA: I am Ra. It is well that the appliances for the arms were placed upon the instrument. We ask that continued vigilance be accorded these distortions, which are, if anything, more distorted towards disease than at our previous cautionary statement.

All is well, my friends. You are conscientious and faithful in your alignments. We appreciate your fastidiousness.

I am Ra. I leave you now, rejoicing merrily in the love and the light of the One Infinite Creator. Go forth, then, rejoicing in the power and in the peace of the One Infinite Creator. Adonai.

Session 91,
June 26, 1982

RA: I am Ra. I greet you in the love and in the light of the One Infinite Creator. We communicate now.

QUESTIONER: Could you first please give me the condition of the instrument?

RA: I am Ra. It is as previously stated.

QUESTIONER: I have listed the different minds and would like to know if they are applied in this particular aspect: first, we have the cosmic mind, which is, I would think, the same for all sub-Logoi like our sun. Is this correct?

RA: I am Ra. This is correct.

QUESTIONER: A sub-Logos such as our sun, then, in creating Its own particular evolutionary experience, refines the cosmic mind or, shall we say, articulates it by Its own additional bias or biases. Is this the correct observation?

RA: I am Ra. It is a correct observation with the one exception that concerns the use of the term "addition," which suggests the concept of that which is more than the all-mind. Instead, the archetypical mind is a refinement of the all-mind in a pattern peculiar to the sub-Logo's choosing.

QUESTIONER: Then the very next refinement that occurs as the cosmic mind is refined is what we call the archetypical mind. Is this correct?

RA: I am Ra. Yes.

QUESTIONER: Then this creates, I would assume, the planetary or racial mind. Is this correct?

RA: I am Ra. No.

QUESTIONER: What is the origin of the planetary or racial mind?

RA: I am Ra. This racial or planetary mind is, for this Logos, a repository of biases remembered by the mind/body/spirit complexes which have enjoyed the experience of this planetary influence.

QUESTIONER: Now, some entities on this planet evolved from second density into third, and some were transferred from other planets to recycle in third density here. Did the ones who were transferred here to recycle in third density add to the planetary or racial mind?

RA: I am Ra. Not only did each race add to the planetary mind, but also each race possesses a racial mind. Thus we made this distinction in discussing this portion of mind. This portion of mind is formed in the series of seemingly non-simultaneous experiences which are chosen in freedom of will by the mind/body/spirit complexes of the planetary influence. Therefore, although this Akashic, planetary, or racial mind is indeed a root of mind, it may be seen in sharp differentiation from the deeper roots of mind which are not a function of altering memory, if you will.

We must ask your patience at this time. This channel has become somewhat unclear due to the movement of the cover which touches this instrument. We ask that the opening sentences be repeated and the breath expelled.

[The microphones attached to the cover upon the instrument were pulled slightly as a rug was being placed over a noisy tape recorder. The Circle of One was walked, breath was expelled 2 feet above the instrument's head from her right to her left, and the Circle of One was walked again as requested.]

RA: I am Ra. We communicate now.

QUESTIONER: Were we successful in re-establishing clear contact?

RA: I am Ra. There was the mis-step which then needed to be rere-peated. This was done. The communication is once again clear. We enjoyed the humorous aspects of the necessary repetitions.

QUESTIONER: What occurred when the microphone cords were slightly moved?

RA: I am Ra. The link between the instrument's mind/body/spirit complex and its yellow-ray, chemical, physical vehicle was jarred. This caused some maladjustment of the organ you call the lungs, and, if the repair had not been done, would have resulted in a distorted physical-complex condition of this portion of the instrument's physical vehicle.

QUESTIONER: What kind of distortion?

RA: I am Ra. The degree of distortion would depend upon the amount of neglect. The ultimate penalty, shall we say, for the disturbing of the physical vehicle is the death, in this case by what you would call the congestive heart failure. As the support group was prompt, there should be little or no distortion experienced by the instrument.

QUESTIONER: Why does such a very minor effect like the slight movement of the microphone cord result in this situation, not mechanically or chemically, but philosophically, if you can answer this question?

RA: I am Ra. We can only answer mechanically as there is no philosophy to the reflexes of physical vehicular function.

There is what you might call the silver-cord reflex; that is, when the mind/body/spirit complex dwells without the environs of the physical shell and the physical shell is disturbed, the physical shell will reflexively call back the absent enlivener; that is, the mind/body/spirit complex, which is connected with what may be metaphysically seen as what some of your philosophers have called the silver cord. If this is done suddenly, the mind/body/spirit complex will attempt entry into the energy web of the physical vehicle without due care, and the effect is as if one were to stretch one of your elastic bands and let it shrink rapidly. The resulting snap would strike hard at the anchored portion of the elastic band.

The process through which you as a group go in recalling this instrument could be likened unto taking this elastic and gently lessening its degree of tension until it was without perceptible stretch.

QUESTIONER: To get back to what we were talking about, would the different races of this planet be from different planets in our local vicinity or the planets of nearby Logoi which have evolved through their second-density experiences, and would they create the large number of different races that we experience on this planet?

RA: I am Ra. There are correctnesses to your supposition. However, not all races and sub-races are of various planetary origins. We suggest that in looking at planetary origins, one observes not the pigmentation of the integument but the biases concerning interactions with other-selves and definitions regarding the nature of the self.

QUESTIONER: How many different planets have supplied the individuals which now inhabit this planet?

RA: I am Ra. This is perceived by us to be unimportant information, but harmless. There are three major planetary influences upon your planetary sphere, besides those of your own second-density derivation, and thirteen minor planetary groups in addition to the above.

QUESTIONER: Thank you. One more question before we start on the specific questions in regard to archetypes. Do all Logoi evolving after the veil have twenty-two archetypes?

RA: I am Ra. No.

QUESTIONER: Is it common for Logoi to have twenty-two archetypes, or is this relatively unique to our Logos?

RA: I am Ra. The system of sevens is the most articulated system yet discovered by any experiment by any Logos in our octave.

QUESTIONER: What is the largest number of archetypes, to Ra's knowledge, used by a Logos?

RA: I am Ra. The sevens plus The Choice is the greatest number which has been used, by our knowledge, by Logoi. It is the result of many, many previous experiments in articulation of the One Creator.

QUESTIONER: I assume, then, that twenty-two is the greatest number of archetypes. I also ask is it the minimum number presently in use by any Logos, to Ra's knowledge?

RA: I am Ra. The fewest are the two systems of five which are completing the cycles or densities of experience.

You must grasp the idea that the archetypes were not developed at once but step by step, and not in order as you know the order at this space/time but in various orders. Therefore, the two systems of fives were using two separate ways of viewing the archetypical nature of all experience. Each, of course, used the Matrix, the Potentiator, and the Significator, for this is the harvest with which our creation began.

One way or system of experimentation had added to these the Catalyst and the Experience. Another system, if you will, had added Catalyst and Transformation. In one case, the methods whereby experience was processed was further aided, but the fruits of experience less aided. In the second case, the opposite may be seen to be the case.

QUESTIONER: Thank you. We have some observations on the archetypes, which are as follows. First, the Matrix of the Mind is depicted in the Egyptian Tarot by a male, and this we take as creative energy intelligently directed. Will Ra comment on this?

RA: I am Ra. This is an extremely thoughtful perception, seeing as it does the male not specifically as biological male but as a male principle. You will note that there are very definite sexual biases in the images. They are intended to function both as information as to which biological entity or energy will attract which archetype, and also as a more general view which sees polarity as a key to the archetypical mind of third density.

QUESTIONER: The second observation is that we have a wand that has been seen as the power of the will. Will Ra comment?

RA: I am Ra. The concept of will is indeed pouring forth from each facet of the image of the Matrix of the Mind. The wand as the will, however, is, shall we say, an astrological derivative of the outreaching hand forming the, shall we say, magical gesture. The excellent portion of the image which may be seen distinctly as separate from the concept of the wand is that sphere which indicates the spiritual nature of the object of the will of one wishing to do magical acts within the manifestation of your density.

QUESTIONER: The hand downward has been seen as seeking from within and not from without, and the active dominance over the material world. Would Ra comment on that?

RA: I am Ra. Look again, O student. Does the hand reach within? Nay. Without potentiation, the conscious mind has no inwardness. That hand, O student, reaches towards that which, outside its unpotentiated influence, is locked from it.

QUESTIONER: The square cage represents the material illusion and is an unmagical shape. Can Ra comment on that?

RA: I am Ra. The square, wherever seen, is the symbol of the third-density illusion and may be seen either as unmagical or, in the proper configuration, as having been manifested within; that is, the material world given life.

QUESTIONER: The dark area around the square, then, would be the darkness of the subconscious mind. Would Ra comment on that?

RA: I am Ra. There is no further thing to say to the perceptive student.
QUESTIONER: The checkered portion would represent polarity?
RA: I am Ra. This also is satisfactory.

QUESTIONER: The bird is a messenger, which the hand is reaching down to unlock. Can Ra comment on that?

RA: I am Ra. The winged visions or images in this system are to be noted not so much for their distinct kind as for the position of the wings. All birds are indeed intended to suggest that just as the Matrix figure, the Magician, cannot act without reaching its winged spirit, so neither can the spirit fly, lest it be released into conscious manifestation and fructified thereby.

QUESTIONER: The star would represent the potentiating forces of the subconscious mind. Is this correct?

RA: I am Ra. This particular part of this image is best seen in astrological terms. We would comment at this space/time that Ra did not include the astrological portions of these images in the system of images designed to evoke the archetypical leitmotifs.

QUESTIONER: Are there any other additions to Card Number One other than the star that are of other than the basic archetypical aspects?

RA: I am Ra. There are details of each image seen through the cultural eye of the time of inscription. This is to be expected. Therefore, when viewing the, shall we say, Egyptian costumes and systems of mythology used in the images, it is far better to penetrate to the heart of the costumes' significance or the creatures' significance rather than clinging to a culture which is not your own.

In each entity the image will resonate slightly differently. Therefore, there is the desire upon Ra's part to allow for the creative envisioning of each archetype, using general guidelines rather than specific and limiting definitions.

QUESTIONER: The cup represents a mixture of positive and negative passions. Could Ra comment on that?

RA: I am Ra. The otic portions of this instrument's physical vehicle did not perceive a significant portion of your query. Please requery.

QUESTIONER: There is apparently a cup which we have as containing a mixture of positive and negative influences. However, I personally doubt this. Could Ra comment on this, please?

RA: I am Ra. Doubt not the polarity, O student, but release the cup from its stricture. It is indeed a distortion of the original image.

QUESTIONER: What was the original image?

RA: I am Ra. The original image had the checkering as the suggestion of polarity.

QUESTIONER: Then was this a representation of the waiting polarity to be tasted by the Matrix of the Mind?

RA: I am Ra. This is exquisitely perceptive.

QUESTIONER: I have listed here the sword as representing struggle. I am not sure that I even can call anything in this diagram a sword. Would Ra comment on that?

RA: I am Ra. Doubt not the struggle, O student, but release the sword from its stricture. Observe the struggle of a caged bird to fly.

QUESTIONER: I have listed the coin represents work accomplished. I am also in doubt about the existence of the coin in this diagram. Could Ra comment on that please?

RA: I am Ra. Again, doubt not that which the coin is called to represent, for does not the Magus strive to achieve through the manifested world? Yet release the coin from its stricture.

QUESTIONER: And finally, the Magician represents the conscious mind. Is this correct?

RA: I am Ra. We ask the student to consider the concept of the unfed conscious mind, the mind without any resource but consciousness. Do not confuse the unfed conscious mind with that mass of complexities which you as students experience, as you have so many, many times dipped already into the processes of potentiation, catalyst, experience, and transformation.

QUESTIONER: Are these all of the components, then, of this first archetype?

RA: I am Ra. These are all you, the student, see. Thusly the complement is complete for you. Each student may see some other nuance. We, as we have said, did not offer these images with boundaries but only as guidelines intending to aid the adept and to establish the architecture of the deep, or archetypical, portion of the deep mind.

QUESTIONER: How is the knowledge of the facets of the archetypical mind used by the individual to accelerate his evolution?

RA: I am Ra. We shall offer an example based upon this first-explored archetype or concept complex. The conscious mind of the adept may be full to bursting of the most abstruse and unimaginable of ideas, so that further ideation becomes impossible, and work in blue ray or indigo is blocked through over-activation. It is then that the adept would call upon the new mind, untouched and virgin, and dwell within the archetype of the new and unblemished mind without bias, without polarity, full of the magic of the Logos.

QUESTIONER: Then you are saying, if I am correct in understanding what you have just said, that the conscious mind may be filled with an almost infinite number of concepts, but there is a set of basic concepts which are what I would call important simply because they are the foundations for the evolution of consciousness, and will, if carefully applied, accelerate the evolution of consciousness, whereas the vast array of concepts, ideas, and experiences that we meet in our daily lives may have little or no bearing upon the evolution of consciousness except in a very indirect way. In other words, what we are attempting to do here is find the motivators of evolution and utilize them to move through our evolutionary track. Is this correct?

RA: I am Ra. Not entirely. The archetypes are not the foundation for spiritual evolution but rather are the tool for grasping in an undistorted manner the nature of this evolution.

QUESTIONER: So for an individual who wished to consciously augment his own evolution, an ability to recognize and utilize the archetypes would be beneficial in sorting out that which he wishes to seek from that which would be not as efficient a seeking tool. Would this be a good statement?

RA: I am Ra. This is a fairly adequate statement. The term "efficient" might also fruitfully be replaced by the term "undistorted." The archetypical mind, when penetrated lucidly, is a blueprint of the builded structure of all energy expenditures and all seeking without distortion. This, as a resource within the deep mind, is of great potential aid to the adept.

We would ask for one more query at this space/time, as this instrument is experiencing continuous surges of the distortion you call pain, and we wish to take our leave of the working while the instrument still possesses a sufficient amount of transferred energy to ease the transition to the waking state, if you would call it that.

QUESTIONER: Since we are at the end of the Matrix of the Mind, I will just ask if there is anything that we can do to make the instrument more comfortable or to improve the contact.

RA: I am Ra. Each is most conscientious. The instrument might be somewhat more comfortable with the addition of the swirling of the waters with spine erect. All other things which can be performed for the instrument's benefit are most diligently done. We commend the continual fidelity of the group to the ideals of harmony and thanksgiving. This shall be your great protection. All is well, my friends. The appurtenances and alignments are excellent.

I am Ra. I leave you glorying in the love and in the light of the One Infinite Creator. Go forth, then, rejoicing in the power and the peace of the One Infinite Creator. Adonai.

Session 92,
July 8, 1982

RA: I am Ra. I greet you in the love and in the light of the One Infinite Creator. We communicate now.

QUESTIONER: Could you first please give me the condition of the instrument?

RA: I am Ra. The condition of this instrument is slightly more distorted towards weakness in each respect since the previous asking.

QUESTIONER: Is there a specific cause for this, and could you tell us what it is?

RA: I am Ra. The effective cause of the increased physical distortions has to do with the press of continuing substantial levels of the distortion you call pain. Various vehicular distortions other than the specifically arthritic have been accentuated by psychic greeting, and the combined effect has been deleterious.

The continued slight but noticeable loss of the vital energies is due to the necessity for the instrument to call upon this resource in order to clear the, shall we say, way for a carefully purified service-to-others working. The use of the will in the absence of physical and, in this particular case, mental and mental/emotional energies requires vital energies.

QUESTIONER: We have been trying to figure out how to provide the instrument with the swirling waters, and we hope to do that soon. Is there any other thing that we can do to improve this situation?

RA: I am Ra. Continue in peace and harmony. Already the support group does much. There is the need for the instrument to choose the manner of its beingness. It has the distortion, as we have noted, towards the martyrdom. This can be evaluated and choices made only by the entity.

QUESTIONER: What is the present situation with the negative fifth-density visitor?

RA: I am Ra. It is with this group.

QUESTIONER: What prompted it to return?

RA: I am Ra. The promptings were duple. There was the recovery of much negative polarity upon the part of your friend of fifth density, and at the same approximate nexus a temporary lessening of the positive harmony of this group.

QUESTIONER: Is there anything that we can do about the instrument's stomach problem or constipation?

RA: I am Ra. The healing modes of which each is capable are already in use.

QUESTIONER: In the last session we discussed the first Tarot card of the Egyptian type. Are there any distortions in the cards that we have that Ra did not originally intend, or any additions that Ra did intend in this particular Tarot?

RA: The distortions remaining after the removal of astrological material are those having to do with the mythos of the culture to which Ra offered this teach/learning tool. This is why we have suggested approaching the images looking for the heart of the image rather than being involved overmuch by the costumes and creatures of a culture not familiar to your present incarnation. We have no wish to add to an already distorted group of images, feeling that although distortion is inevitable, there is the least amount which can be procured in the present arrangement.

QUESTIONER: Then you are saying that the cards that we have here are the best available cards.

RA: I am Ra. Your statement is correct in that we consider the so-called Egyptian Tarot the most undistorted version of the images which Ra offered. This is not to intimate that other systems may not, in their own way, form an helpful architecture for the adept's consideration of the archetypical mind.

QUESTIONER: I would like to make an analogy of when a baby is first born. I am assuming that the Matrix of the Mind is new and undistorted and veiled from the Potentiator of the Mind and ready for that which it is to experience in the incarnation. Is this correct?

RA: I am Ra. Yes.

QUESTIONER: I will read several statements and ask for Ra's comments. The first is: Until an entity becomes consciously aware of the evolutionary process, the Logos or intelligent energy creates the potentials for an entity to gain the experience necessary for polarization. Would Ra comment on that?

RA: I am Ra. This is so.

QUESTIONER: Then, this occurs because the Potentiator of the Mind is directly connected, through the roots of the tree of mind, to the archetypical mind and to the Logos which created it, and because the veil between the Matrix and Potentiator of the Mind allows for the development of the will. Will Ra comment on that?

RA: I am Ra. Some untangling may be needed. As the mind/body/spirit complex which has not yet reached the point of the conscious awareness of the process of evolution prepares for incarnation, it has programmed for it a less than complete—that is to say, a partially randomized—system of learnings. The amount of randomness of potential catalyst is proportional to the newness of the mind/body/spirit complex to third density. This, then, becomes a portion of that which you may call a potential for incarnational experience. This is indeed carried within that portion of the mind which is of the deep mind, the architecture of which may be envisioned as being represented by that concept complex known as the Potentiator.

It is not in the archetypical mind of an entity that the potential for incarnational experience resides, but in the mind/body/spirit complex's insertion, shall we say, into the energy web of the physical vehicle and the chosen planetary environment. However, to more deeply articulate this portion of the mind/body/spirit complex's beingness, this archetype, the Potentiator of the Mind, may be evoked with profit to the student of its own evolution.

QUESTIONER: Then are you saying that the source of pre-incarnatively programmed catalyst is the Potentiator of the Mind?

RA: I am Ra. No. We are suggesting that the Potentiator of the Mind is an archetype which may aid the adept in grasping the nature of this pre-incarnative and continuingly incarnative series of choices.

QUESTIONER: The third statement: Just as free will taps intelligent infinity, which yields intelligent energy, which then focuses and creates the densities of this octave of experience, the Potentiator of the Mind utilizes its connection with intelligent energy and taps or potentiates the Matrix of the Mind, which yields the Catalyst of the Mind. Is this correct?

RA: I am Ra. This is thoughtful but confused. The Matrix of the Mind is that which reaches just as the kinetic phase of intelligent infinity, through free will, reaches for the Logos, or, in the case of the mind/body/spirit complex, the sub-sub-Logos which is the free-will-potentiated beingness of the mind/body/spirit complex; to intelligent infinity, Love, and all that follows from that Logos; to the Matrix or, shall we say, the conscious, waiting self of each entity, the Love or the sub-sub-Logos spinning through free will all those things which may enrich the experience of the Creator by the Creator.

It is indeed so that the biases of the potentials of a mind/body/spirit complex cause the catalyst of this entity to be unique and to form a coherent pattern that resembles the dance, full of movement, forming a many-figured tapestry of motion.

QUESTIONER: The fourth statement: When the Catalyst of the Mind is processed by the entity, the Experience of the Mind results. Is this correct?

RA: I am Ra. There are subtle misdirections in this simple statement, having to do with the overriding qualities of the Significator. It is so that catalyst yields experience. However, through free will and the faculty of imperfect memory, catalyst is most often only partially used and the experience thus correspondingly skewed.

QUESTIONER: Then, the dynamic process between the Matrix, Potentiator, Catalyst, and Experience of the Mind forms the nature of the mind or the Significator of the Mind. Is this correct?

RA: I am Ra. As our previous response suggests, the Significator of the Mind is both actor and acted upon. With this exception, the statement is largely correct.

QUESTIONER: As the entity becomes consciously aware of this process, it programs this activity itself before the incarnation. Is this correct?

RA: I am Ra. This is correct. Please keep in mind that we are discussing not the archetypical mind, which is a resource available equally to each but unevenly used, but that to which it speaks: the incarnational experiential process of each mind/body/spirit complex. We wish to make this distinction clear, for it is not the archetypes which live the incarnation but the conscious mind/body/spirit complex which may indeed live the incarnation without recourse to the quest for articulation of the processes of potentiation, experience, and transformation.

QUESTIONER: Thank you. And finally, as each energy center becomes activated and balanced, the Transformation of the Mind is called upon more and more frequently. When all of the energy centers are activated and balanced to a minimal degree, contact with intelligent infinity occurs, the veil is removed, and the Great Way of the Mind is called upon. Is this correct?

RA: I am Ra. No. This is a quite eloquent look at some relationships within the archetypical mind. However, it must be seen once again that the archetypical mind does not equal the acting incarnational mind/body/spirit complex's progression or evolution.

Due to the first misperception, we hesitate to speak to the second consideration but shall attempt clarity. While studying the archetypical mind, we may suggest that the student look at the Great Way of the Mind, not as that which is attained after contact with intelligent infinity, but rather as that portion of the archetypical mind which denotes and configures the particular framework within which the Mind, the Body, or the Spirit archetypes move.

QUESTIONER: Turning, then, to my analogy or example of the newborn infant and its undistorted Matrix of the Mind, this newborn infant has its subconscious mind veiled from the Matrix of the Mind. The second archetype, the Potentiator of the Mind, is going to act at some time through the veil—though I hesitate to say through the veil, since I don't think that is a very good way of stating it—but the Potentiator of the Mind will act to create a condition such as the example I mentioned of the infant touching a hot object. The hot object we could take as random catalyst. The infant can either leave its hand on the hot object or rapidly remove it. My question is, is the Potentiator of the Mind involved at all in this experience, and, if so, how?

RA: I am Ra. The Potentiator of Mind and of Body are both involved in the questing of the infant for new experience. The mind/body/spirit complex which is an infant has one highly developed portion which may be best studied by viewing the Significators of Mind and Body. You notice we do not include the spirit. That portion of a mind/body/spirit complex is not reliably developed in each and every mind/body/spirit complex. Thusly the infant's significant self, which is the harvest of biases of all previous incarnational experiences, offers to this infant biases with which to meet new experience.

However, the portion of the infant which may be articulated by the Matrix of the Mind is indeed unfed by experience and has the bias of reaching for this experience through free will, just as intelligent energy in the kinetic phase, through free will, creates the Logos. These sub-sub-Logoi, then, or those portions of the mind/body/spirit complex which may be articulated by consideration of the Potentiators of Mind and Body, through free will, choose to make alterations in their experiential continuum. The results of these experiments in novelty are then recorded in the portion of the mind and body articulated by the Matrices thereof.

QUESTIONER: Are all activities that the entity has from the state of infancy a function of the Potentiator of the Mind?

RA: I am Ra. Firstly, although the functions of the mind are indeed paramount over those of the body, the body being the creature of the mind, certainly not all actions of a mind/body/spirit complex could be seen to be due to the potentiating qualities of the mind complex alone, as the body and in some cases the spirit also potentiates action.

Secondly, as a mind/body/spirit complex becomes aware of the process of spiritual evolution, more and more of the activities of the mind and body which precipitate activity are caused by those portions of the mind/body/spirit complex which are articulated by the archetypes of Transformation.

QUESTIONER: The Matrix of the Mind is depicted as a male on the card, and the Potentiator as female. Could Ra state why this is, and how this affects these two archetypes?

RA: I am Ra. Firstly, as we have said, the Matrix of the Mind is attracted to the biological male, and the Potentiator of the Mind to the biological female. Thusly, in energy transfer the female is able to potentiate that which may be within the conscious mind of the male so that it may feel enspirited.

In a more general sense, that which reaches may be seen as a male principle. That which awaits the reaching may be seen as a female principle. The richness of the male and female system of polarity is interesting and we would not comment further but suggest consideration by the student.

QUESTIONER: In card #2, the Potentiator of the Mind, we see a female seated on a rectangular block. She is veiled and sitting between two pillars, which seem to be identically covered with drawings, but one is much darker than the other. I am assuming that the veil represents the veil between the conscious and subconscious or Matrix and Potentiator of the Mind. Is this correct?

RA: I am Ra. This is quite correct.

QUESTIONER: I am assuming that she sits between the different-colored columns, with the dark one on her left, to indicate at this position an equal opportunity for the potentiation of the mind to be of the negative or positive nature. Would Ra comment on this?

RA: I am Ra. Although this is correct, it is not as perceptive as the notice that the Priestess, as this figure has been called, sits within a structure in which polarity, symbolized as you correctly noted by the light and dark pillars, is an integral and necessary part. The unfed mind has no polarity just as intelligent infinity has none. The nature of the sub-sub-sub-Logos which offers the third-density experience is one of polarity, not by choice but by careful design.

We perceive an unclear statement. The polarity of Potentiator is there not for the Matrix to choose. It is there for the Matrix to accept as given.

QUESTIONER: In other words, this particular illusion has polarity as its foundation, which might be represented by the structural significance of these columns. Is this correct?

RA: I am Ra. This is correct.

QUESTIONER: It seems to me that the drawings on each of these columns are identical, but that the left-hand column—that is, the one on the Priestess's left—has been shaded much darker, indicating that the events and the experiences may be identical in the incarnation but may be approached, viewed, and utilized with either polarity. Is this correct?

RA: I am Ra. This is correct. You will note also, from the symbol denoting spirit in manifestation upon each pillar, that the One Infinite Creator is no respecter of polarity but offers Itself in full to all.

QUESTIONER: There seems to be a book on the Priestess's lap which is half hidden by a robe or material that covers her right shoulder. It would seem that this indicates that knowledge is available if the veil is lifted but is not only hidden by the veil but is hidden partially by her very garment, which she must somehow remove to become aware of the knowledge which she has available. Is this correct?

RA: I am Ra. In that the conceit of the volume was not originated by Ra, we ask that you release the volume from its strictured form. Your perceptions are quite correct.

The very nature of the feminine principle of mind, which, in Ra's suggestion, was related specifically to what may be termed sanctified sexuality, is, itself, without addition, the book which neither the feminine nor the male principle may use until the male principle has reached and penetrated, in a symbolically sexual fashion, the inner secrets of this feminine principle.

All robes, in this case indicating the outer garments of custom, shield these principles. Thusly there is great dynamic tension, if you will, betwixt the Matrix and the Potentiator of the Mind.

QUESTIONER: Are there any other parts of this picture that were not given by Ra?

RA: I am Ra. The astrological symbols offered are not given by Ra.

QUESTIONER: The fact that the Priestess sits atop the rectangular block indicates to me that the Potentiator of the Mind has dominance or is above the material illusion. Is this in any way correct?

RA: I am Ra. Let us say, rather, that this figure is immanent, near at hand, shall we say, within all manifestation. The opportunities for the reaching to the Potentiator are numerous. However, of itself the Potentiator does not enter manifestation.

QUESTIONER: Would the half moon on the crown represent the receptivity of the subconscious mind?

RA: I am Ra. This symbol is not given by Ra, but it is not distasteful, for within your own culture the moon represents the feminine, the sun the masculine. Thusly we accept this portion as a portion of the image, for it seems without significant distortion.

QUESTIONER: Was the symbol on the front of the Priestess's shirt given by Ra?

RA: I am Ra. The crux ansata is the correct symbol. The addition and slight distortion of this symbol thereby is astrological and may be released from its stricture.

QUESTIONER: Would this crux ansata then be indicating the sign of life as the spirit enlivening matter?

RA: I am Ra. This is quite correct. Moreover, it illuminates a concept which is a portion of the archetype which has to do with the continuation of the consciousness which is being potentiated, in incarnation, beyond incarnation.

QUESTIONER: Were the grapes depicted on the cloth over her shoulder of Ra's communication?

RA: I am Ra. Yes.

QUESTIONER: We have those as indicating the fertility of the subconscious mind. Is that correct?

RA: I am Ra. This is correct, O student, but note ye the function of the mantle. There is great protection given by the very character of potentiation. To bear fruit is a protected activity.

QUESTIONER: The protection here seems to be depicted as being on the right-hand side but not the left. Would this indicate that there is protection for the positive path but not for the negative?

RA: I am Ra. You perceive correctly an inborn bias offering to the seeing eye and listing ear information concerning the choice of the more efficient polarity. We would at this time, as you may call it, suggest one more full query.

QUESTIONER: I will attempt an example of the Potentiator of the Mind acting. As the infant gains time in incarnation, would it experience the Potentiator offering both positive and negative potential thoughts, shall I say, for the Matrix to experience, which then begin to accumulate in the Matrix and color it one way or the other in polarity depending upon its continuing choice of that polarity? Is this in any way correct?

RA: I am Ra. Firstly, again may we distinguish between the archetypical mind and the process of incarnational experience of the mind/body/spirit complex.

Secondly, each potentiation which has been reached for by the Matrix is recorded by the Matrix but experienced by the Significator. The experience of the Significator of this potentiated activity is of course dependent upon the acuity of its processes of Catalyst and Experience.

May we ask if there are briefer queries before we leave this instrument?

QUESTIONER: Is there anything that we can do to make the instrument more comfortable or to improve the contact?

RA: I am Ra. The support group is functioning well. The instrument, itself, might ponder some earlier words and consider their implications. We say this because the continued calling upon vital energies, if allowed to proceed to the end of the vital energy, will end this contact. There is not the need for continued calling upon these energies. The instrument must find the key to this riddle or face a growing loss of this particular service at this particular space/time nexus.

All is well. The alignments are exemplary.

I am Ra. I leave you, my friends, in the love and the light of the

One Infinite Creator. Go forth, then, rejoicing in the power and in the peace of the One Infinite Creator. Adonai.

Session 93,
August 18, 1982

RA: I am Ra. I greet you in the love and in the light of the One Infinite Creator. We communicate now.

QUESTIONER: Could you first please give me the condition of the instrument?

RA: I am Ra. The physical complex distortions of this instrument far more closely approach what you might call the zero mark; that is, the instrument, while having no native physical energy, is not nearly so far in physical energy-deficit distortions. The vital-energy distortions are somewhat strengthened since the last asking.

QUESTIONER: What is the position and condition of our fifth-density, negatively oriented visitor?

RA: I am Ra. This entity is with this group but in a quiescent state due to some bafflement as to the appropriate method for enlarging upon its chosen task.

QUESTIONER: Thank you. You have stated previously that the foundation of our present illusion is the concept of polarity. I would like to ask, since we have defined the two polarities as service to others and service to self, is there a more complete or eloquent or enlightening definition of these polarities or any more information that we don't have at this time that you could give on the two ends of the poles that would give us a better insight into the nature of polarity itself?

RA: I am Ra. It is unlikely that there is a more pithy or eloquent description of the polarities of third density than service to others and service to self, due to the nature of the mind/body/spirit complexes' distortions towards perceiving concepts relating to philosophy in terms of ethics or activity. However, we might consider the polarities using slightly variant terms. In this way a possible enrichment of insight might be achieved for some.

One might consider the polarities with the literal nature enjoyed by the physical polarity of the magnet. The negative and positive, with electrical characteristics, may be seen to be just as in the physical sense. It is to be noted in this context that it is quite impossible to judge the polarity of an act or an entity, just as it is impossible to judge the relative goodness of the negative and positive poles of the magnet.

Another method of viewing polarities might involve the concept of radiation/absorption. That which is positive is radiant; that which is negative is absorbent.

QUESTIONER: Now, if I understand correctly, prior to the veiling process the electrical polarities, the polarities of radiation and absorption, all existed in some part of the creation, but the service-to-others/service-to-self polarity with which we are familiar had not evolved and only showed up after the veiling process as an addition to the list of possible polarities in the creation. Is this correct?

RA: I am Ra. No.

QUESTIONER: Would you correct me on that?

RA: I am Ra. The description of polarity as service to self and service to others, from the beginning of our creation, dwelt within the architecture of the primal Logos. Before the veiling process, the impact of actions taken by mind/body/spirits upon their consciousness was not palpable to a significant enough degree to allow the expression of this polarity to be significantly useful. Over the period of what you would call time, this expression of polarity did indeed work to alter the biases of mind/body/spirits so that they might eventually be harvested. The veiling process made the polarity far more effective.

QUESTIONER: I might make the analogy, then, in that when a polarization in the atmosphere occurs to create thunderstorms, lightning, and much activity, this more vivid experience could be likened to the polarization in consciousness which creates the more vivid experience. Would this be appropriate as an analogy?

RA: I am Ra. There is a shallowness to this analogy in that one entity's attention might be focused upon a storm for the duration of the storm. However, the storm-producing conditions are not constant, whereas the polarizing conditions are constant. Given this disclaimer, we may agree with your analogy.

QUESTIONER: With the third Tarot card we come to the first addition of archetypes after the veiling process, as I understand it. I am assuming that this third archetype is, shall I say, loaded in a way so as to create the possible polarization, since that seems to be one of the primary objectives of this particular Logos in the evolutionary process. Am I in any way correct on that?

RA: I am Ra. Before we reply to your query, we ask your patience as we must needs examine the mind complex of this instrument in order that we might attempt to move the left manual appendage of the instrument. If we are not able to effect some relief from pain, we shall take our leave. Please have patience while we do that which is appropriate.

[Thirty-second pause]

I am Ra. There will continue to be pain flares. However, the critical portion of the intense pain has been alleviated by repositioning.

Your supposition is correct.

QUESTIONER: There seems to be no large hint of polarity in this drawing except for the possible coloration of the many cups in the wheel. Part of them are colored black, and part are colored white. Would this indicate that each experience has within it the possible negative or positive use of that experience that is randomly generated by this seeming wheel of fortune?

RA: I am Ra. Your supposition is thoughtful. However, it is based upon an addition to the concept complex which is astrological in origin. Therefore, we request that you retain the concept of polarity but release the cups from their strictured form. The element you deal with is not in motion in its original form but is indeed the abiding sun, which, from the spirit, shines in protection over all catalyst available from the beginning of complexity to the discerning mind/body/spirit complex.

Indeed, you may, rather, find polarity expressed, firstly, by the many opportunities offered in the material illusion which is imaged by the not-white and not-dark square upon which the entity of the image is seated, secondly, upon the position of that seated entity. It does not meet opportunity straight on but glances off to one side or another. In the image you will note a suggestion that the offering of the illusion will often seem to suggest the opportunities lying upon the left-hand path or, as you might refer to it more simply, the service-to-self path. This is a portion of the nature of the Catalyst of the Mind.

QUESTIONER: The feet of the entity seem to be on an unstable platform that is dark to the rear and light to the front. I am guessing that possibly this indicates that the entity standing on this could sway in either direction, to the left- or to the right-hand path. Is this correct?

RA: I am Ra. This is most perceptive.

QUESTIONER: The bird, I am guessing, might be a messenger of the two paths depicted by the position of the wings, bringing catalyst which could be used to polarize on either path. Is this in any way correct?

RA: I am Ra. It is a correct perception that the position of the winged creature is significant. The more correct perception of this entity and its significance is the realization that the mind/body/spirit complex is, having made contact with its potentiated self, now beginning its flight towards that great Logos which is that which is sought by the adept.

Further, the nature of the winged creature is echoed both by the female holding it and the symbol of the female upon which the figure's feet rest; that is, the nature of catalyst is overwhelmingly of an unconsciousness, coming from that which is not of the mind and which has no connection with the intellect, as you call it, which precedes or is concomitant with catalytic action. All uses of catalyst by the mind are those consciously applied to catalyst. Without conscious intent, the use of catalyst is never processed through mediation, ideation, and imagination.

QUESTIONER: I would like, if possible, an example of the activity we call Catalyst of the Mind in a particular individual undergoing this process. Could Ra give an example of that?

RA: I am Ra. All that assaults your senses is catalyst. We, in speaking to this support group through this instrument, offer catalyst. The configurations of each in the group of body offer catalyst through comfort/discomfort. In fact, all that is unprocessed that has come before the notice of a mind/body/spirit complex is catalyst.

QUESTIONER: Then presently we receive catalyst of the mind as we are aware of Ra's communication, and we receive catalyst of the body as our bodies sense all of the inputs to them, but could Ra then describe catalyst of the spirit, and are we at this time receiving that catalyst, and, if not, could Ra give an example of that?

RA: I am Ra. Catalyst being processed by the body is catalyst for the body. Catalyst being processed by the mind is catalyst for the mind. Catalyst being processed by the spirit is catalyst for the spirit. An individual mind/body/spirit complex may use any catalyst which comes before its notice, be it through the body and its senses or through mediation or through any other more highly developed source, in its unique way to form an experience unique to it, with its biases.

QUESTIONER: Would I be correct in saying that the archetype for the Catalyst of the Mind is the Logos's model for its most efficient plan for the activity or use of the catalyst of the mind?

RA: I am Ra. Yes.

QUESTIONER: Then the adept, in becoming familiar with the Logos's archetype in each case, would be able to most efficiently use the Logos's plan for evolution. Is this correct?

RA: I am Ra. In the archetypical mind, one has the resource of not specifically a plan for evolution but rather a blueprint or architecture of the nature of evolution. This may seem to be a small distinction, but it has significance in perceiving more clearly the use of this resource of the deep mind.

QUESTIONER: Then Ra presented the images which we know now as the Tarot, so that the Egyptian adepts of the time could accelerate their personal evolution. Is this correct, and was there any other reason for the presentation of these images by Ra?

RA: I am Ra. You are correct.

QUESTIONER: Are there any other uses at all of Tarot cards other than the one I just named?

RA: I am Ra. To the student, the Tarot images offer a resource for learn/teaching the processes of evolution. To any other entity, these images are pictures and no more.

QUESTIONER: I was specifically thinking of the fact that Ra, in an earlier session, spoke of the Tarot as a system of divination. Would you tell me what you meant by that?

RA: I am Ra. Due to the influence of the Chaldees, the system of archetypical images was incorporated by the priests of that period into a system of astrologically based study, learning, and divination. This was not a purpose for which Ra developed the Tarot.

QUESTIONER: The third card also shows the wand, I am assuming it is, in the right hand. The ball atop the wand is the round magical shape. Am I in any way correct in guessing that the Catalyst of the Mind suggests the possible eventual use of the magic depicted by this wand?

RA: I am Ra. The wand is astrological in its origin and as an image may be released from its stricture. The sphere of spiritual power is an indication indeed that each opportunity is pregnant with the most-extravagant magical possibilities for the far-seeing adept.

QUESTIONER: The fact that the clothing of the entity is transparent indicates the semipermeability of the veil for the catalytic process. Is this correct?

RA: I am Ra. We again must pause.

[Fifteen-second pause]

I am Ra. We continue under somewhat-less-than-optimal conditions. However, due to the nature of this instrument's opening to us, our pathway is quite clear and we shall continue. Because of pain flares, we must ask you to repeat your last query.

QUESTIONER: I was just wondering if the transparency of the garments on the third card indicates the semipermeable nature of the veil between the conscious and unconscious mind.

RA: I am Ra. This is a thoughtful perception and cannot be said to be incorrect. However, the intended suggestion, in general, is an echo of our earlier suggestion that the nature of catalyst is that of the unconscious; that is, outward catalyst comes through the veil.

All that you perceive seems to be consciously perceived. This is not the correct supposition. All that you perceive is perceived as catalyst unconsciously. By the, shall we say, time that the mind begins its appreciation of catalyst, that catalyst has been filtered through the veil, and in some cases much is veiled in the most apparently clear perception.

QUESTIONER: I'm at a loss to know the significance of the serpents that adorn the head of the entity on this drawing. Are they of Ra, and, if so, what do they stand for?

RA: I am Ra. They are cultural in nature. In the culture to which these images were given, the serpent was the symbol of wisdom. Indeed, to the general user of these images, perhaps the most accurate connotation of this portion of the concept complexes might be the realization that the serpent is that which is powerful magically. In the positive sense this means that the serpent will appear at the indigo-ray site upon the body of the image figures. When a negative connotation is intended, one may find the serpent at the solar plexus center.

QUESTIONER: Is there any significance to the serpent? Is there any polarity to the serpent as we experience it in this illusion?

RA: I am Ra. We assume that you question the serpent as used in these images rather than the second-density life form which is a portion of your experience. There is a significance to the serpent form in a culture which coexists with your own but which is not your own; that is, the serpent is symbol of that which some call the kundalini and which we have discussed in previous material.

QUESTIONER: Is there any other aspect of this third card that Ra could comment on at this time?

RA: I am Ra. There may be said to be many aspects which another student might note and ponder in this image. However, it is the nature of teach/learning to avoid trespass into the realms of learn/teaching for the student. We are quite agreed to comment upon all observations that the student may make. We cannot speak further than this for any student.

We would add that it is expected that each student shall naturally have an unique experience of perception dealing with each image. Therefore, it is not expected that the questioner ask comprehensively for all students. It is, rather, expected and accepted that the questioner will ask a moiety of questions which build up a series of concepts concerning each archetype, which then offer to each succeeding student the opportunity for more-informed study of the archetypical mind.

May we ask for one more query at this time. We are pleased to report that this instrument has remembered to request the reserving of some transferred energy to make more comfortable the transition back to the waking state. Therefore, we find that there is sufficient energy for one more query.

QUESTIONER: I am assuming that you mean one full question. I'll make that question in this form. I'd like to know the significance of the shape of the crux ansata, and if that's too much of an answer, I'll just ask if there is anything that we can do to make the instrument more comfortable or to improve the contact?

RA: I am Ra. There are mathematical ratios within this image which may yield informative insights to one fond of riddles. We shall not untangle the riddle. We may indicate that the crux ansata is a part of the concept complexes of the archetypical mind, the circle indicating the magic of the spirit, the cross indicating that nature of manifestation which may only be valued by the losing. Thus the crux ansata is intended to be seen as an image of the eternal in and through manifestation and beyond manifestation through the sacrifice and the transformation of that which is manifest.

The support group functions well. The swirling waters experienced by the instrument since our previous working have substantially aided the instrument in its lessening of the distortion of pain.

All is well. The alignments are well guarded.

We leave you, my friends, in the love and the light of the Infinite One. Go forth, therefore, rejoicing in the power and in the peace of the One Infinite and Glorious Creator. Adonai.

Session 94,
August 26, 1982

RA: I am Ra. I greet you in the love and in the light of the One Infinite Creator. I communicate now.

QUESTIONER: Could you first please give me the condition of the instrument?

RA: I am Ra. There is some small increase in physical-energy deficit. It is not substantial. All else is as at the previous asking.

QUESTIONER: From the previous session the statement was made that much is veiled to the most apparently clear observation. Would Ra expand on what was meant by that statement? I assume that this means the veiling of all that which is outside the limits of what we call our physical perception having to do with the spectrum of light, etc., but I also intuit that there is more than that veiled. Would Ra expand on that concept?

RA: I am Ra. You are perceptive in your supposition. Indeed, we meant not any suggestions that the physical apparatus of your current illusion was limited as part of the veiling process. Your physical limits are as they are.

However, because of the unique biases of each mind/body/spirit complex, there are sometimes quite simple instances of distortion when there is no apparent cause for such distortion. Let us use the example of the virile and immature male who meets and speaks clearly with a young female whose physical form has the appropriate configuration to cause, for this male entity, the activation of the red-ray sexual arousal.

The words spoken may be upon a simple subject such as naming, information as to the occupation, and various other common interchanges of sound vibratory complex. The male entity, however, is using almost all the available consciousness it possesses in registering the desirability of the female. Such may also be true of the female.

Thusly an entire exchange of information may be meaningless because the actual catalyst is of the body. This is unconsciously controlled and is not a conscious decision. This example is simplistic.

QUESTIONER: I have drawn a small diagram in which I simply show an arrow which represents catalyst penetrating a line at right angles to the arrow, which is the veil, depositing in one of two repositories which I would call the right-hand path and the left-hand path, and I have labeled these two repositories the Experience. Would this be a very rough analogy of the way the catalyst is filtered through the veil to become experience?

RA: I am Ra. Again, you are partially correct. The deeper biases of a mind/body/spirit complex pilot the catalyst around the many isles of positivity and negativity as expressed in the archipelago of the deeper mind. However, the analogy is incorrect in that it does not take into account the further polarization which most certainly is available to the conscious mind after it has perceived the partially polarized catalyst from the deeper mind.

QUESTIONER: It seems to me that the Experience of the Mind would act in such a way as to change the nature of the veil so that catalyst would be filtered so as to be acceptable in the bias that is increasingly chosen by the entity. For instance, if he had chosen the right-hand path, the Experience of the Mind would change the permeability of the veil to accept more and more positive catalyst. Also, the other would be true for accepting more negative catalyst if the left-hand path were the one that was chosen. Is this correct?

RA: I am Ra. This is not only correct, but there is a further ramification. As the entity increases in experience, it shall, more and more, choose positive interpretations of catalyst if it is upon the service-to-others path, and negative interpretations of catalyst if its experience has been of the service-to-self path.

QUESTIONER: Then the mechanism designed by the Logos of the action of catalyst resulting in experience was planned to be self-accelerating, in that it would create this process of variable permeability. Is this an adequate statement?

RA: I am Ra. There is no variable permeability involved in the concepts we have just discussed. Except for this, you are quite correct.

QUESTIONER: Now I can understand, to use a poor term again, the necessity for the archetype of Catalyst of the Mind, but what is the reason for having a blueprint or model for the Experience of the Mind other than this simple model of dual repositories for negative and positive catalyst? It seems to me that the first distortion of free will would be better served if no model for experience was made. Could you clear that up for me?

RA: I am Ra. Your question is certainly interesting and your confusion hopefully productive. We cannot learn/teach for the student. We shall simply note, as we have previously, the attraction of various archetypes to male and to female. We suggest that this line of consideration may prove productive.

QUESTIONER: In the fourth archetype the card shows a male whose body faces forward. I assume that this indicates that the Experience of the Mind will reach for catalyst. However, the face is to the left, which indicates to me that in reaching for catalyst, negative catalyst will be more apparent in its power and effect. Would Ra comment on this?

RA: I am Ra. The archetype of Experience of the Mind reaches not, O student, but, with firm authority, grasps what it is given. The remainder of your remarks are perceptive.

QUESTIONER: The Experience is seated upon the square of the material illusion which is colored much darker than in Card Number Three. However, there is a cat inside this square. I am guessing that as experience is gained, the second-density nature of the illusion is understood and the negative and positive aspects separate. Would Ra comment on this?

RA: I am Ra. This interpretation varies markedly from Ra's intention. We direct the attention to the cultural meaning of the great cat which guards. What, O student, does it guard? And with what oriflamme does it lighten that darkness of manifestation? The polarities are, indeed, present; the separation nonexistent except through the sifting which is the result of cumulative experience. Other impressions were intended by this configuration of the seated image with its milk-white leg and its pointed foot.

QUESTIONER: In Card Number Three the feet of the female entity are upon the unstable platform, signifying the dual polarity by its color. In Card Number Four, one foot is pointed so that if the male entity stands on the toe it would be carefully balanced. The other foot is pointed to the left. Would Ra comment on my observation that if the entity stands on this foot, it will be very, very carefully balanced?

RA: I am Ra. This is an important perception, for it is a key to not only this concept complex but to others as well. You may see the T square, which, at times riven as is one foot from secure fundament by the nature of experience yet still by this same nature of experience, is carefully, precisely, and architecturally placed in the foundation of this concept complex and, indeed, in the archetypical mind complex. Experience[7] has the nature of more effectively and poignantly expressing the architecture of experience, both the fragility of structure and the surety of structure.

QUESTIONER: It would seem to me, from the configuration of this male entity in Card Number Four, who looks to the left with the right foot pointed to the left, that this card would indicate you must be in a defensive position with respect to the left-hand path, but there is no need to concern yourself about protection with respect to the right-hand path. Would Ra comment on that?

---

7. i.e., Card Number Four

RA: I am Ra. Again, this is not the suggestion we wished to offer by constructing this image. However, the perception cannot be said to be incorrect.

QUESTIONER: The magical shape is on the right edge of the Card Number Four, which indicates to me that the spiritual experience would be on the right-hand path. Could Ra comment on that?

RA: I am Ra. Yes. The figure is expressing the nature of experience by having its attention caught by what may be termed the left-hand catalyst. Meanwhile, the power, the magic, is available upon the right-hand path.

The nature of experience is such that the attention shall be constantly given varieties of experience. Those that are presumed to be negative, or interpreted as negative, may seem in abundance. It is a great challenge to take catalyst and devise the magical, positive experience. That which is magical in the negative experience is much longer coming, shall we say, in the third density.

QUESTIONER: Both the third and fourth archetypes, as I see it, work together for the sole purpose of creating the polarity in the most efficient manner possible. Is this correct?

RA: I am Ra. This cannot be said to be incorrect. We suggest contemplation of this thought complex.

QUESTIONER: Then prior to the veiling process, that which we call catalyst after the veiling was not catalyst simply because it was not efficiently creating polarity, because this loading process, you might say, that I have diagrammed, of catalyst passing through the veil and becoming polarized experience, was not in effect because the viewing of what we call catalyst by the entity was seen much more clearly as the experience of the One Creator and not something that was a function of other mind/body/spirit complexes. Would Ra comment on that statement?

RA: I am Ra. The concepts discussed seem without significant distortion.

QUESTIONER: Thank you. Then we're expecting, in Card Number Four, to see the result of catalytic action and, therefore, a greater definition between the dark and the light areas. In just glancing at this card, we notice that it is more definitely darkly colored in some areas and more white in others in a general sense than in Card Number Three, indicating to me that the separation along the two biases has occurred and should occur in order to follow the blueprint for experience. Could Ra comment on that?

RA: I am Ra. You are perceptive, O student.

QUESTIONER: The bird in Card Number Three now seems to be internalized in the center of the entity in Card Number Four, in that it has changed from its flight in Card Number Three. The flight has achieved its objective and has become a part, a central part, of the experience. Could Ra comment on that?

RA: I am Ra. This perception is correct, O student, but what shall the student find the bird to signify?

QUESTIONER: I would guess that the bird signifies that a communication that comes as catalyst signified in Card Number Three is accepted by the female and, used, becomes a portion of the experience. I'm not sure of that at all. Am I in any way correct?

RA: I am Ra. That bears little of sense.

QUESTIONER: I'll have to work on that.
Then I am guessing that the crossed legs of the entity in Card Four have a meaning similar to the crux ansata. Is this correct?

RA: I am Ra. This is correct. The cross formed by the living limbs of the image signifies that which is the nature of mind/body/spirit complexes in manifestation within your illusion. There is no experience which is not purchased by effort of some kind, no act of service to self or others which does not bear a price, to the entity manifesting, commensurate with its purity. All things in manifestation may be seen in one way or another to be offering themselves in order that transformations may take place upon the level appropriate to the action.

QUESTIONER: The bird is within the circle on the front of the entity on Card Four. Would that have the same significance of the circular part of the crux ansata?

RA: I am Ra. It is a specialized form of this meaningful shape. It is specialized in great part due to the nature of the crossed legs of manifestation, which we have previously discussed.

QUESTIONER: The entity on Card Four wears a strangely shaped skirt. Is there a significance to the shape of this skirt?

RA: I am Ra. Yes.

QUESTIONER: The skirt is extended toward the left hand but is somewhat shorter toward the right. There is a black bag hanging from the belt of the entity on the left side. It seems to me that this black bag has a meaning of the acquiring of the material possessions of wealth as a part of the left-hand path. Would Ra comment on that?

RA: I am Ra. Although this meaning was not intended by Ra as part of this complex of concepts, we find the interpretation quite acceptable.

[Thirty-second pause]

I am Ra. As we observe a lull in the questioning, we shall take this opportunity to say that the level of transferred energy dwindles rapidly, and we would offer the opportunity for one more full question at this working, if it is desired.

QUESTIONER: I would just state that this card, being male, would indicate that as experience is gained, the mind becomes the motivator or that which reaches or does more than the simple experiencer it was prior to the gaining of the catalytic action. There is a greater tendency for the mind to direct the mind/body/spirit complex, and other than that, I would just ask if there is anything that we can do to make the instrument more comfortable or to improve the contact.

RA: I am Ra. In the context of your penultimate query, we would suggest that you ponder again the shape of the garment which the image wears. Such habiliment is not natural. The shape is significant and is so along the lines of your query.

The support group cares well for the instrument. We would ask that care be taken, as the instrument has been offered the gift of a distortion towards extreme cold by the fifth-density friend which greets you.

Although you may be less than pleased with the accoutrements, may we say that all was as carefully prepared as each was able. More than that, none can do. Therefore, we thank each for the careful alignments. All is well.

We leave you, my friends, in the love and in the light of the One

Glorious Infinite Creator. Go forth, then, rejoicing in the power and in the peace of the One. Adonai.

Session 95,
September 2, 1982

RA: I am Ra. I greet you, my friends, in the love and in the light of the One Infinite Creator. We communicate now.

QUESTIONER: Could you first please give me the condition of the instrument?

RA: I am Ra. It is as previously stated.

QUESTIONER: Thank you. What is the situation with respect to our fifth-density negative associate?

RA: I am Ra. The aforenamed entity has chosen various means to further its service, and though each is effective in itself, none leads to the lessening of the dedication to service for others or the valuing of harmonious interaction. Therefore, the entity, though not quiet as it has been, is somewhat depolarized on balance.

QUESTIONER: There seems to be an extremely high probability that we will move from this position to another residence. If we move from this residence and cease using this room for workings with Ra, is there a magically appropriate ritual for closing the use of this place of working, or is there anything that we should do with respect to leaving this particular place?

RA: I am Ra. It would be appropriate to remove from this room and, to a lesser extent, from the dwelling, the charging of what you might call the distortion towards sanctity. To remove this charge, it is valuable either to write upon your paper your own working or to use existing rituals for the deconsecration of a sacred place such as one of your churches.

QUESTIONER: Thank you. The new room that we choose for this working will of course be carefully cleaned, and marred surfaces made well. We shall also use the Banishing Ritual of the Lesser Pentagram prior to a working. Is there anything else that Ra could suggest? I would like, also, to know if there is anything in particular that you might suggest with respect to the particular place that has been chosen for our new location.

RA: I am Ra. We scan the recent memory configurations of the questioner. Firstly, there have been some less-than-harmonious interactions within this dwelling. The dynamics of this interaction were potent enough to attract a lesser thought-form. Therefore, we suggest the salting and ritual cleansing by blessed water of all windows and doorways which offer adit into the domicile or any outbuildings thereof.

Further, we suggest the hanging of the cut garlic clove in the portion of the room which has accommodated those whose enjoyment has turned into a darker emotion, centering upon the area we find you call the wet bar, also the room intended for the sleeping which is found near the kitchen area. The appropriate words used to bid farewell to those of the lower astral shall be used in connection with the hanging of the garlic cloves for the period of approximately thirty-six of your hours. We believe that this is equivalent to two of your night periods and one of your lit periods. This should cleanse the house as you find it, to the extent that it is neutral in its vibrations of harmony, love, and thanksgiving which this group shall then, as the incarnational experience proceeds, offer to the domicile.

QUESTIONER: I am assuming that we would prepare the blessed water the same as we prepare the water for the instrument to drink after a session, and would then wipe the windows and doors with this water. This would probably have to be done in a bucket. I would like to know if this is correct, and what was meant by salting the windows and doors?

RA: I am Ra. Firstly, you may bless the water yourselves or may request so-called holy water from any blessed place; that is, blessed by intention. Secondly, the water shall be carefully shaken from the fingers along the sills of all windows and doors as they have been opened. Thirdly, prior to the sprinkling of this cleansing, blessing sacrament of water, the salt shall be trailed along these sills in a line and again allowed to exist in this configuration for thirty-six to forty-eight hours. Then the virgin broom may ritually sweep the salt out of each window and doorway, sweeping with each stroke the less fortunate of the vibrations within the dwelling which might find coexistence with the group difficult.

QUESTIONER: I assume that you mean that we should put the salt only on the outer doorway sills and not on the inner doorway sills in the house. Is that correct?

RA: I am Ra. This is correct. We cannot express the nature of salt and water and garlic with clarity enough to inform you as to the efficacy with which salt absorbs vibrations which have been requested to move into salt when salt has been given water. We cannot express the full magical nature of your water, nor can we express the likeness and attractiveness of the garlic cut to lower astral forms. The attractiveness is negative, and no service-to-self astral form will accept coexistence with the cut garlic.

Therefore, we offer the suggestions. We also request, carefully, that the broom be clean and that the garlic be burned. The virginity of the broom is most efficacious.

QUESTIONER: Let me see if I have the scenario correctly in mind. I'll repeat my version of it. We would hang fresh-cut garlic in the area of the wet bar and in the area of the bedroom that is adjacent to the kitchen area. We would salt all window sills and all outer-wall door sills and then sprinkle blessed water from our fingers on the salted areas. We would then say the appropriate words to bid farewell to lower astrals. Those words I am not sure of. Would Ra comment on the scenario that I have stated?

RA: I am Ra. Your grasp of our suggestions is good. We note that the salt be poured in the straight line with no gaps. There are various ritual words of blessing and farewell to entities such as you are removing. We might suggest the following.

When the salt is laid, you may repeat, "We praise the One Creator which gave to salt the ability to enable those friends, to which we wish to bid farewell, to find a new home."

As the water is sprinkled, you may say, "We give thanks to the One Creator for the gift of water. Over it the Creator moves Its hand and stirs Its will to be done."

The hanging of the cut garlic may be accompanied by the words "We praise the One Creator for the gift of garlic and bless its ability to offer to those friends to whom we wish to bid farewell the arrow which points their way of egress."

When the sweeping is done, you may say, "We praise the One Creator and give thanksgiving for the spiritual cleanliness of this dwelling place."

As the garlic is burned, you may say, "We give thanks to the One Creator for the gift of spiritual cleanliness in our dwelling place and seal the departure of all those who have left by this exit by the consuming of this substance."

QUESTIONER: Is there any place more appropriate than any other to hang the garlic in the room; for instance, over the windows or anything like that? I know that it is supposed to be hung in the area of the bar, but I meant in the bedroom. Is there any more appropriate place than another?

RA: I am Ra. The windows and the doorways are most appropriate, and, in addition, we suggest the salting and sprinkling of any door which may lead elsewhere than out of the dwelling, in order to afford to the entities the understanding that they are not desired elsewhere within the dwelling.

QUESTIONER: I understand that the garlic is to be used at the bar area and the bedroom that is close to the kitchen and has an exit onto the carport. If I am correct, those are the only two places that it is to be used. This is correct, isn't it?

RA: I am Ra. This is correct.

QUESTIONER: We would like to pick the most appropriate room for sanctifying for the Ra contact. Is there any room that would be most appropriate that Ra could name?

RA: I am Ra. When you have finished with your work, the dwelling shall be as a virgin dwelling in the magical sense. You may choose that portion of the dwelling that seems appropriate, and once having chosen it you may then commence with the same sort of preparation of the place with which you have been familiar here in this dwelling place.

QUESTIONER: I am assuming that the newly chosen place meets the parameters for the best contact with Ra on the exterior of the house, and I would like to ask Ra at this time if there are any suggestions with respect to the exterior of the house.

RA: I am Ra. The dwelling seems surrounded with the trees and fields of your countryside. This is acceptable. We suggest the general principle of preparing each part of your environment as it best suits each in the group with the beauty which each may feel to be appropriate. There is much of blessing in the gardening and the care of surroundings, for when this is accomplished in love of the creation, the second-density flowers, plants, and small animals are aware of this service and return it.

QUESTIONER: On one end of the house are four stalls that have been occupied by horses. Would it be appropriate or necessary to modify in any way the condition of that area even though it is outside the living area?

RA: I am Ra. There has been no undesirable negative energy stored in this area. Therefore, it is acceptable if physically cleaned.

QUESTIONER: Is there any other comment about our new location that Ra could make?

RA: I am Ra. We are gratified that this query was offered to us, for there has been a concentration of negative thought patterns at a distance north to 10° of north, approximately 45 of what you call yards extending therefrom to all four directions in a rectangular but irregular shape.

We ask that the garlic be strung approximately 60–70 feet beyond the far verge of this area, which is approximately 57 yards from the dwelling on a bearing north to 10° of north. We suggest that the garlic be hung in the funnel so that the energies are drawn into the south small end of the funnel and traduced northward and away from the dwelling. The procedure of the hanging will be one for testing your ingenuity, but there are several ways to suspend the substance, and it is well to do so.

QUESTIONER: I envision a cardboard funnel approximately 3 feet in length, and then a small cardboard of the same configuration inside of that funnel, the garlic placed between the two cardboard surfaces so that the garlic actually makes a funnel itself, held in place by the two cardboard cones. The smaller end of the cone would be toward the house, and the larger end would be away from the house.

I would also like to know that I am accurately aware of the position that we are talking about. Taking a specific point on the house such as the front door, I suspect that the direction is up toward the road that leads out of the property. An exact measurement from the doorknob to the center of the area of negativity of which we speak would be helpful. Would Ra comment on that?

RA: I am Ra. We were working from the other side of the dwelling. However, the exact distance is not important due to the generalized nature of the astral leavings. The heading would be approximately 10° east of north to 5° east of north. This is not a heading in which absolute fastidiousness needs be paramount. The yardage is approximately as given. As to the hanging of the garlic, it must be able to be blown by the wind. Therefore, the structure which was envisioned is less than optimal. We might suggest the stringing between two placed posts on either side of the funnel of the strung cloves.

QUESTIONER: Would a wire framework such as chicken wire which has a small inch-square mesh or something like that shaped into a cone, with the garlic attached to the cone, with the small end toward the house and the open end away from the house, strung between two poles, be appropriate?

RA: I am Ra. That is appropriate. You see in this case the center of the negativity is as described, but there will be a general cleansing of the dwelling and its acreage by this means. One action you might take in order to improve the efficacy of the cleansing of the environment is the walking of the perimeter with the opened clove in hand, swinging the clove. No words need be said unless each wishes to silently or verbally speak those words given for garlic previously.

QUESTIONER: Is there any other thing that we can do to prepare this new place that Ra could mention at this time?

RA: I am Ra. There are no more-specific suggestions for the specific location you contemplate. In general, the cleanliness is most helpful. The removal from the mind complex of those thoughts not of harmony is most helpful, and those practices which increase faith and will that the spirit may do its work are most helpful.

QUESTIONER: After the suggestions are accomplished with respect to cleansing of the property, does Ra anticipate our contact with Ra will be as efficient there as in this particular place?

RA: I am Ra. All places in which this group dwells in love and thanksgiving are acceptable to us.

QUESTIONER: Thank you. A question has been asked which I will ask at this time. In processing the catalyst of dreams, is there a universal language of the unconscious mind which may be used to interpret dreams, or does each entity have a unique language in its own unconscious mind which it may use to interpret the meaning of dreams?

RA: I am Ra. There is what might be called a partial vocabulary of the dreams, due to the common heritage of all mind/body/spirit complexes. Due to each entity's unique incarnational experiences, there is an overlay which grows to be a larger and larger proportion of the dream vocabulary as the entity gains experience.

QUESTIONER: Thank you. In the last session you indicated in the statement about the immature male meeting the immature female that the information exchanged was quite different with respect to what occurred because of the veil. Would you give an example of the information exchange prior to the veil for the same case?

RA: I am Ra. Given this same case—that is, the random red-ray sexual arousal being activated in both male and female—the communication would far more likely have been to the subject of the satisfying of that red-ray sexual impulse. When this had occurred, other information such as the naming could be offered with clear perception. It is to be noted that the catalyst which may be processed by the pre-veil experience is insignificant compared to the catalyst offered to the thoroughly bemused male and female after the veil. The confusion which this situation, simplistic though it is, offers is representative of the efficiency of the enlargement of the catalytic processes occurring after the veiling.

QUESTIONER: For the condition of meeting after the veiling process, either entity will choose, as a function of its previous biases or Card Four, the experience and the way in which it will handle the situation with respect to polarity, therefore probably producing more catalyst for itself along the chosen path of polarization. Would Ra comment on this statement?

RA: I am Ra. This statement is correct.

QUESTIONER: In Card Four, in the last session we spoke of the shape of the skirt, and it has occurred to us that the skirt of the entity representing the archetype of the Experience of the Mind is extended to the left to indicate that other-selves would not be able to get close to this entity if it had chosen the left-hand path. There would be a greater separation between it and other-selves, whereas if it had chosen the right-hand path, there would be much less of a separation. Would Ra comment on that observation?

RA: I am Ra. The student is perceptive.

QUESTIONER: And it seems that the square upon which the entity sits, which is almost totally black, is a representation of the material illusion, and the white cat is guarding the right-hand path, which is now separated in experience from the left. Would Ra comment on that observation?

RA: I am Ra. O student, your sight almost sees that which was intended. However, the polarities need no guardians. What, then, O student, needs the guard?

QUESTIONER: What I meant to say was that the entity is guarded along the right-hand path, once it has chosen this path, from effects of the material illusion that are of the negative polarity. Would Ra comment on that?

RA: I am Ra. This is an accurate perception of our intent, O student. We may note that the great cat guards in direct proportion to the purity of the manifestations of intention and the purity of inner work done along this path.

QUESTIONER: From that statement I interpret the following. If the Experience of the Mind has sufficiently chosen the right-hand path, and as total purity is approached in the choosing of the right-hand path, then total imperviousness from the effect of the left-hand catalyst is also approached. Is this correct?

RA: I am Ra. This is exquisitely perceptive. The seeker which has purely chosen the service-to-others path shall certainly not have a variant apparent incarnational experience. There is no outward shelter in your illusion from the gusts, flurries, and blizzards of quick and cruel catalyst.

However, to the pure, all that is encountered speaks of the love and the light of the One Infinite Creator. The cruelest blow is seen with an ambiance of challenges offered and opportunities to come. Thusly, the great pitch of light is held high above such an one so that all interpretation may be seen to be protected by light.

QUESTIONER: I have often wondered about the action of random and programmed catalyst with respect to the entity with the very strong positive or negative polarization. Would either polarity be free to a great extent from random catalyst such as great natural catastrophes or warfare or something like that which generates a lot of random catalyst in the physical vicinity of a highly polarized entity? Does this great cat, then, have an effect on such random catalyst on the right-hand path?

RA: I am Ra. In two circumstances this is so. Firstly, if there has been the pre-incarnative choice that, for instance, one shall not take life in the service of the cultural group, events shall fall in a protective manner. Secondly, if any entity is able to dwell completely in unity, the only harm that may occur to it is the changing of the outward physical, yellow-ray vehicle into the more light-filled mind/body/spirit complex's vehicle by the process of death. All other suffering and pain is as nothing to one such as this.

We may note that this perfect configuration of the mind, body, and spirit complexes, while within the third-density vehicle, is extraordinarily rare.

QUESTIONER: Am I to understand, then, that there is no protection at all if the Experience of the Mind has chosen the left-hand path and that path is traveled? All random catalyst may affect the negatively polarized individual as a function of the statistical nature of the random catalyst. Is this correct?

RA: I am Ra. This is correct. You may note some of those of your peoples which, at this space/time nexus, seek places of survival. This is due to the lack of protection when service to self is invoked.

QUESTIONER: The possibility of the legs of the entity of Card Four being at right angles was linked with the tesseract,[8] mentioned in a much earlier session by Ra, as the direction of transformation from space/time into time/space, and I was thinking that possibly it was also linked with the crux ansata. Am I in any way correct in this observation?

RA: I am Ra. This shall be the last query of this working, as transferred energy wanes. The observation of the right angles and their transformational meaning is most perceptive, O student. Each of the images leading to the Transformations of Mind, Body, and Spirit and ultimately to the great transformative Choice has the increasing intensity of increasing articulation of concept; that is to say, each image in which you find this angle may increasingly be seen to be a more and more stridently calling voice of opportunity to use each resource, be it experience as you now observe or further images, for the grand work of the adept which builds towards transformation using the spirit's bountiful shuttle to intelligent infinity. Please ask any brief queries at this space/time.

---

8. tesseract: in speculative mathematics, a cube which has developed at least one additional dimension.

QUESTIONER: Is there anything that we can do to make the instrument more comfortable or to improve the contact?

RA: I am Ra. We observe some small worsening of the distortions of the dorsal side. This is due to the nature of the beginning use of the swirling waters. The difficulties are physically accentuated as the swirling waters begin to aid the musculature surrounding the nexi of distortions. We encourage the swirling waters and note that complete immersion in them is somewhat more efficacious than the technique now used.

We ask that the support group attempt to aid the instrument in remembering to preserve the physical energies and not expend them upon movements associated with the packing, as you call this activity, and the movement between geographical locations upon your sphere.

The alignments are excellent. All is well.

We leave you glorying in the love and in the light of the One Infinite Creator. Go forth, therefore, rejoicing in the mighty peace of the One Infinite Creator. Adonai.

Session 96,
September 9, 1982

RA: I am Ra. I greet you in the love and in the light of the One Infinite Creator. We communicate now.

QUESTIONER: Could you first please give me the condition of the instrument?

RA: I am Ra. The physical-energy deficit is significantly greater than the last asking. There has been substantive lessening also of the vital energies, although the perquisite degree of energy for mental/emotional distortions of normalcy are yet available.

QUESTIONER: The instrument asks if the house which is to be our new location is capable of being transformed by painting and cleaning. We don't plan to put down all new carpets. Would cleaning the carpets that are there now be acceptable?

I want to bring this particular house up to acceptable limits so that it is neutral after we do the salting. I have a concern only for the conditions for our work there. The physical location isn't that important. In fact, I don't consider that important at all. Could Ra comment on this?

RA: I am Ra. It is, of course, the preference of this group which is the only consideration in the situation for the contact with Ra. The domicile in question has already been offered a small amount of blessing by this group through its presence, and, as we have previously stated, each of your days spent in love, harmony, and thanksgiving will continue transforming the dwelling.

It is correct, as we have previously stated, that physical cleanliness is most important. Therefore, the efforts shall be made to most thoroughly cleanse the dwelling. In this regard it is to be noted that neither in the dwelling as a whole wherein you now reside or in the chamber of this working is there an absence of your dust, earth, and other detritus which is in toto called dirt. If the intention is to clean, as much as is physically possible, the location, the requirements for physical cleanliness are fulfilled. It is only when a lower astral entity has, shall we say, placed portions of itself in the so-called dirt that care should be taken to remove the sentient being. These instructions we have given.

May we note that just as each entity strives in each moment to become more nearly one with the Creator but falls short, just so is physical spotlessness striven for but not achieved. In each case the purity of intention and thoroughness of manifestation are appreciated. The variance between the attempt and the goal is never noted and may be considered unimportant.

QUESTIONER: The sequence of events that I am considering is first the painting and then the cleaning, then the moving in of the furniture, then the salting and use of garlic. Is this as good as any other sequence, or would another sequence be better?

RA: I am Ra. Any sequence which results in the cleansing is acceptable. It is to be noted that the thresholds are not to be crossed during the cleansing. Since such stricture upon use of the limen may affect your considerations, we make note of this.

QUESTIONER: Would Ra comment on the technique of blessing the water that we will use to sprinkle the salt? I assume that we just sprinkle the water directly off of our finger tips onto the line of salt. How much water, in general, should be sprinkled on the salt? How wet should we get it? I would like to get this done right.

RA: I am Ra. The blessing of the water may be that one we have previously given, or it may be that one which is written within the liturgy of this instrument's distortion of the worship of the One Creator, or it may simply be obtained from what you call your Catholic Church in the form of holy water.

The intention of blessing is the notable feature of blessed water. The water may be sprinkled not so that all salt is soaked but so that a goodly portion has been dampened. This is not a physical working. The substances need to be seen in their ideal state so that water may be seen to be enabling the salt.

QUESTIONER: I have planned to redraw the Tarot cards, omitting the extraneous additions by those who came after Ra, and I would like quickly to go through those things that I intend to eliminate from each card and ask Ra if there is anything else that should be eliminated to make the cards as they were before the astrological and other appendages were added.

I would eliminate all of the letters from the edge of the card, with the possible exception of the number of the card. That would be the case for all of the cards. In Card Number One I would eliminate the star and the wand in the Magician's hand, and I understand that the sphere remains, but I am not really sure where it should be. Would Ra comment on that please?

RA: I am Ra. Firstly, the elimination of letters is acceptable.

Secondly, the elimination of stars is acceptable in all cases.

Thirdly, the elimination of the wand is appropriate.

Fourthly, the sphere may be seen to be held by the thumb and index and second finger.

Fifthly, we would note that it is not possible to offer what you may call a pure deck, if you would use this term, of Tarot due to the fact that when these images were first drawn, there was already distortion in various and sundry ways, mostly cultural.

Sixthly, although it is good to view the images without the astrological additions, it is to be noted that the more general positions, phases, and characteristics of each concept complex are those which are significant. The removal of all distortions is unlikely and, to a great extent, unimportant.

QUESTIONER: I didn't think that we could ever remove all distortions, but it is very difficult to work with or interpret these cards because of the quality of the drawing, and as we go through them we get a better idea of what some of these things are and how they should be drawn. I think that we can improve on the quality of the cards and also remove some of the extraneous material that is misleading.

On the second card we should remove the letters and the stars. At the center of the female form here, she is wearing something that looks something like a crux ansata, and we should change that. Is that correct?

RA: I am Ra. We perceive an incomplete query. Please requestion.

QUESTIONER: I think that I should put a crux ansata in the place of this thing that looks a little like a crux ansata on the front of the female. Is that correct?

RA: I am Ra. This is correct.

QUESTIONER: Then as to the thing that she wears on her head, that, I believe, is a bit confusing. What should it be shaped like?

RA: I am Ra. We shall allow the student to ponder this point. We note that although it is an astrologically based addition to the concept complex, it is not entirely unacceptable when viewed with a certain feeling. Therefore, we suggest, O student, that you choose whether to remove the crown or to name its meaning in such a way as to enhance the concept complex.

QUESTIONER: Would Ra please give me any information possible on the ratios of dimensions, and the shape of the crux ansata as it should be made or drawn?

RA: I am Ra. No.

QUESTIONER: In Card Number Three we will remove all the letters and the stars, and I assume that the little cups around the outside of the rays representing the sun should be removed? Is that correct?

RA: I am Ra. Yes.

QUESTIONER: In Card Number Four we will remove all the letters and the stars, and it seems that again we have a situation of removing the wand and putting the sphere in the hand. Is that correct?

RA: I am Ra. Again, this is a matter of choice. Though astrological in nature, this particular scepter has possibilities of relevance in the originally intended concept complex.

This instrument is experiencing some small lack of that distortion which you call proper breathing due to the experience of your near past, as you perceive it. Therefore, as this instrument has requested a substantial enough amount of transferred energy to be retained that it might effect a comfortable re-entry, we shall at this time ask for one more query, after noting the following.

We did not complete our statement upon the dimensions of the crux ansata. It is given in many places. There are decisions to be made as to which drawing of this image is the appropriate one. We may, of course, suggest viewing the so-called Great Pyramid if the puzzle is desired. We do not wish to work this puzzle. It was designed in order that in its own time it be deciphered. In general, of course, this image has the meaning previously stated.

QUESTIONER: Is there anything that we can do to make the instrument more comfortable or to improve the contact?

RA: I am Ra. Continue in harmony, communication, praise, and thanksgiving.

We would note that this instrument's distortions would be lessened were it to refrain from the speaking to some extent for a diurnal period or perhaps two if the difficulty remains. We would also recommend against the activity such as running, which would cause rapid respiration. This aftereffect of the greeting is not necessarily long-lasting. However, as this instrument has some blood vessels in the forward regions of the skull—that is, the integument covering the skull— which are greatly swollen at this time, and since this instrument has the distortion known as the streptococcal infection, it is best to be full of care for a short period in order that the distortions do not catapult the entity into longer-term aftereffects.

All is well. We find the alignments satisfactory.

I am Ra. I leave you in the love and light of the Infinite One. Go forth, therefore, rejoicing in the power and in the peace of the One Infinite Creator. Adonai.

Session 97,
September 15, 1982

RA: I am Ra. I greet you in the love and in the light of the One Infinite Creator. We communicate now.

QUESTIONER: Could you first please give me the condition of the instrument?

RA: I am Ra. It is as previously stated.

QUESTIONER: What is the situation with our fifth-density negative friend?

RA: I am Ra. It is as previously stated.

QUESTIONER: Are there any items in the first four cards not of Ra's intention that we could remove to present a less confusing card as we make our new drawings?

RA: I am Ra. We find much material in this query which would constitute repetition. May we suggest rephrasing the query?

QUESTIONER: Possibly I didn't phrase that the way I meant to. We had already determined the items that should be removed from the first four cards, and my question was this: Had I missed anything that should be removed that was not of Ra's original intention?

RA: I am Ra. We shall repeat our opinion that there are several concepts which, in each image, are astrologically based. However, these concepts are not without merit within the concept complex intended by Ra, given the perception by the student of these concepts in an appropriate manner.

We wish not to form that which may be considered by any mind/body/spirit complex to be a complete and infallible series of images. There is a substantial point to be made in this regard. We have been, with the questioner's aid, investigating the concept complexes of the great architecture of the archetypical mind. To more clearly grasp the nature, the process, and the purpose of archetypes, Ra provided a series of concept complexes. In no way whatsoever should we, as humble messengers of the One Infinite Creator, wish to place before the consideration of any mind/body/spirit complex which seeks its evolution the palest tint of the idea that these images are anything but a resource for working in the area of the development of the faith and the will.

To put this into perspective, we must gaze then at the stunning mystery of the One Infinite Creator. The archetypical mind does not resolve any paradoxes or bring all into unity. This is not the property of any source which is of the third density. Therefore, may we ask the student to look up from inward working and behold the glory, the might, the majesty, the mystery, and the peace of oneness. Let no consideration of bird or beast, darkness or light, shape or shadow, keep any which seeks from the central consideration of unity.

We are not messengers of the complex. We bring the message of unity. In this perspective only may we affirm the value to the seeker of adepthood of the grasping, articulating, and use of this resource of the deep mind exemplified by the concept complex of the archetypes.

QUESTIONER: Thank you. Card Number Five, the Significator of the Mind, indicates, firstly, as I see it, simply a male within a rectangularly structured form which suggests to me that the Significator of the Mind in third density is well bounded within the illusion, as is also suggested by the fact that the base of the male is a rectangular form showing no ability for movement. Would Ra comment on that?

RA: I am Ra. O student, you have grasped the barest essence of the nature of the Significator's complete envelopment within the rectangle. Consider for the self, O student, whether your thoughts can walk. The abilities of the most finely honed mentality shall not be known without the use of the physical vehicle which you call the body. Through the mouth the mind may speak. Through the limbs the mind may effect action.

QUESTIONER: The entity looks to the left, indicating that the mind has the tendency to notice more easily catalyst of a negative essence. Would Ra comment on that observation?

RA: I am Ra. This is substantially correct.

QUESTIONER: There are two small entities at the bottom, one black and one white. I will first ask Ra if this drawing is correct in the coloring. Is the black one in the proper position with respect to Ra's original drawings?

RA: I am Ra. That which you perceive as black was first red. Other than this difference, the beings in the concept complex are placed correctly.

QUESTIONER: The red coloration is a mystery to me. We had originally decided that these represented the polarization of the mind. Would Ra comment on that?

RA: I am Ra. The indications of polarity are as presumed by the questioner. The symbolism of old for the left-hand path was the russet coloration.

We shall pause at this time if the questioner will be patient. There are fairly serious difficulties with the instrument's throat. We shall attempt to ameliorate the situation and suggest the rewalking of the Circle of One.

[The Circle of One was rewalked, and breath expelled 2 feet above the instrument's head.]

RA: I am Ra. Please continue.

QUESTIONER: What was the nature of the problem?

RA: I am Ra. The fifth-density entity which greets this instrument affected a previous difficulty distorting the throat and chest area of the instrument. Some fraction of this distortion remained unmentioned by the instrument. It is helpful if the instrument speaks as clearly as possible to the support group of any difficulties that more care may be taken.

However, we find very little distortion left in the chest area of the instrument. However, immediately preceding the working, the instrument was offered an extreme activation of what you may call the allergies, and the mucous from the flow which this distortion causes began to cause difficulty to the throat. At this juncture the previous potential for the tightening of the throat was somewhat activated by reflex of the yellow-ray, chemical body, over which we have only gross control.

We would appreciate you reminding us to cause this instrument to cough before or after each query for the remainder of this working. Once conscious, this instrument should have no serious difficulty.

QUESTIONER: I was wondering why the dark entity was on the right side of the card in relation to the Significator. Could Ra comment on that after making the instrument cough?

RA: [Cough] The nature of . . . We pause.

[Ten-second pause]

I am Ra. There was a serious pain flare. We may now continue.

The nature of polarity is interesting in that those experiences offered to the Significator as positive frequently become recorded as productive of biases which may be seen to be negative, whereas the fruit of those experiences apparently negative is frequently found to be helpful in the development of the service-to-others bias. As this is perhaps the guiding characteristic of that which the mind processes and records, these symbols of polarity have thusly been placed.

You may note that the hands of the central image indicate the appropriate bias for right- and left-hand working; that is, the right hand gestures in service to others, offering its light outward. The left hand attempts to absorb the power of the spirit and point it for its use alone.

QUESTIONER: The eight cartouches at the bottom would possibly signify the energy centers and the evolution through those centers with the possibility for positive or negative polarization because of the white and black coloration of the figures. Would Ra comment on that after making the instrument cough?

RA: [Cough] I am Ra. The observations of the student are perceptive. It is informative to continue the study of octaves in association with this concept complex. Many are the octaves of a mind/body/spirit complex's beingness. There is not one that does not profit from being pondered in connection with the considerations of the nature of the development of polarity exemplified by the concept complex of your Card Number Five.

QUESTIONER: Do the symbols on the face of each of these little cartouches such as the birds and the other symbols have a meaning in this card that is of value in considering the archetypes? Could you answer that after making the instrument cough?

RA: [Cough] I am Ra. These symbols are letters and words much as your language would receive such an entablature. They are, to a great extent, enculturated by a people not of your generation. Let us, in the rough, suggest that the information written upon these cartouches be understood to be such as the phrase "And you shall be born again to eternal life."

QUESTIONER: Thank you. I thought that the wings on top of the card might indicate the protection of the spirit over the process of evolution. Would Ra comment on that after having the instrument cough?

RA: [Cough] I am Ra. We shall end this session, for we are having considerable difficulty in using the sympathetic nervous system in order to aid the instrument in providing sufficient of your air for its respiration. Therefore, we prematurely suggest ending this session.

Is there any brief query before we leave this instrument?

QUESTIONER: It's not necessary to answer this if you want to end right now for the instrument's benefit, but is there anything that we can do to improve the contact or make the instrument more comfortable?

RA: I am Ra. All is well. The support group functions well.

It is suggested that the instrument be encouraged to take steps to recover completely from the distortion towards the aching of the throat and, to a lesser extent, the chest. There is no way in which we or you may remove that working which has been done. It simply must be removed by physical recovery of the normal distortion. This is not easy due to this instrument's tendency towards allergy.

The alignments are being carefully considered.

I am Ra. I leave you, my friends, glorying and rejoicing in the love and the light of the Infinite Creator. Go forth, then, in the great dance, empowered by the peace of the One Infinite Creator. Adonai.

Session 98, September 24, 1982, contains only personal material and was, for that reason, removed.

Session 99,
November 18, 1982

RA: I am Ra. I greet you in the love and in the light of the One Infinite Creator. We communicate now.

QUESTIONER: Would you please give me the condition of the instrument?

RA: I am Ra. This instrument's physical deficit continues but has the potential for the lessening due to the removal in your probable future of foodstuffs to which the instrument has significant allergy. The vital energy levels are somewhat lessened than the last asking but remain strong. The change in the mental/emotional energy level is towards the distortion of the weakening of this complex.

QUESTIONER: We now have an additional set of Tarot images. Which of these two sets are closer to Ra's original intention?

RA: I am Ra. The principle which moves in accordance with the dynamics of teach/learning with most efficiency is constancy. We could explore the archetypical mind, using that set of images produced by the one known as Fathman, or we could use those which have been used.

In point of fact, those which are being used have some subtleties which enrich the questioning. As we have said, this set of images is not that which we gave. This is not material. We could use any of a multitude of devised Tarot sets. Although this must be at the discretion of the questioner, we suggest the maintaining of one and only one set of distorted images to be used for the querying, and note that the images you now use are good.

QUESTIONER: The wings above Card Five, I am guessing, have to do with a protection over the Significator of the Mind. I am guessing that they are a symbol of protection. Is this in any way correct?

RA: I am Ra. Let us say that you are not incorrect but rather less than correct. The Significator owns a covenant with the spirit which it shall in some cases manifest through the thought and action of the adept. If there is protection in a promise, then you have chosen the correct sound vibration, for the outstretched wings of spirit, high above manifestation, yet draw the caged mind onward.

QUESTIONER: Thank you. In Card Number Six I see the Transformation of the Mind, the male with crossed arms, representing transformation. The transformation is possible either toward the left- or the right-hand path. The path is beckoned or led by the female, the Potentiator. The one on the right has the serpent of wisdom at the brow and is fully clothed, the one on the left having less clothing and indicating that the Potentiator is more concerned or attracted to the physical as the left-hand path is chosen and more concerned and attracted to the mental as the right-hand path is chosen.

The creature above points an arrow at the left-hand path, indicating that if this path is chosen, the chips, shall we say, will fall where they may, the path being unprotected as far as the activity of catalyst. The intellectual abilities of the chooser of the left-hand path would be the main guardian rather than the designed or built-in protection of the Logos for the right-hand path. The entity firing the arrow seems to be a second-density entity, which indicates that this catalyst could be produced by a lesser evolved source, you might say. Would Ra comment on these observations?

RA: I am Ra. We shall speak upon several aspects seriatim.

Firstly, let us examine the crossed arms of the male who is to be transformed. What, O student, do you make of the crossing? What see you in this tangle? There is a creative point to be found in this element which was not discussed overmuch by the questioner.

Let us now observe the evaluation of the two females. The observation that to the left-hand path moves the roughly physical and to the right-hand path the mental has a shallow correctness. There are deeper observations to be made concerning the relationship of the great sea of the unconscious mind to the conscious mind which may fruitfully be pursued. Remember, O student, that these images are not literal. They haunt rather than explicate.

Many use the trunk and roots of mind as if that portion of mind were a badly used, prostituted entity. Then this entity gains from this great storehouse that which is rough, prostituted, and without great virtue. Those who turn to the deep mind, seeing it in the guise of the maiden, go forth to court it. The courtship has nothing of plunder in its semblance and may be protracted, yet the treasure gained by such careful courtship is great. The right-hand and left-hand transformations of the mind may be seen to differ by the attitude of the conscious mind towards its own resources as well as the resources of other-selves.

We now speak of that genie, or elemental, or mythic figure, culturally determined, which sends the arrow to the left-hand transformation. This arrow is not the arrow which kills but rather that which, in its own way, protects. Those who choose separation, that being the quality most indicative of the left-hand path, are protected from other-selves by a strength and sharpness equivalent to the degree of transformation which the mind has experienced in the negative sense. Those upon the right-hand path have no such protection against other-selves, for upon that path the doughty seeker shall find many mirrors for reflection in each other-self it encounters.

QUESTIONER: In the previous session you mentioned the use of the forty-five-minute interval of the tape recorders as a signal for the end of the session. Is this still the appropriate time?

RA: I am Ra. This is, of course, at the discretion of the questioner, for this instrument has some transferred energy and remains open as it has unfailingly done. However, the fragility of the instrument has been more and more appreciated by us. We, in the initial observations, saw the strength of will and overestimated greatly the recuperative abilities of the physical complex of this entity.

Therefore, we may say that ending a working at approximately this amount of energy expenditure—that is, some point soon following upon the sound vibration of which you speak—would be appropriate and, insofar as we may determine, may well extend the incarnational amount of your space/time which this instrument shall be able to offer to this contact.

QUESTIONER: In that case I will just ask this short question as we terminate this session. I want to know if the Logos of this system planned for the mating process as possibly depicted in Card Six—I don't know if this is related to some type of DNA imprinting. In many second-density creatures there seems to be some sort of imprinting that creates a lifetime mating relationship, and I was wondering if this was also carried into third density.

RA: I am Ra. There are some of your second-density fauna which have instinctually imprinted monogamous mating processes. The third-density physical vehicle which is the basic incarnational tool of manifestation upon your planet arose from entities thusly imprinted, all the aforesaid being designed by the Logos.

The free will of third-density entities is far stronger than the rather mild carryover from second-density DNA encoding, and it is not part of the conscious nature of many of your mind/body/spirit complexes to be monogamous due to the exercise of free will. However, as has been noted, there are many signposts in the deep mind indicating to the alert adept the more efficient use of catalyst. As we have said, the Logos of your peoples has a bias towards kindness.

QUESTIONER: Thank you. In closing I will ask if there is anything that we can do to make the instrument more comfortable or to improve the contact?

RA: I am Ra. We note the relative discomfort of this group at this space/time and offer those previous statements made by Ra as possible aids to the regaining of the extraordinary harmony which this group has the capability of experiencing in a stable manner.

We find the addition of the swirling waters to be helpful. The appurtenances are conscientiously aligned.

We encourage the conscious strengthening of those invisible ribbands which fly from the wrists of those who go forward to seek what you may call the Grail. All is well, my friends. We leave you in hopes that each may find true colors to fly in that great metaphysical quest, and urge each to urge each other in love, praise, and thanksgiving.

I am Ra. We leave you in the love and light of the One Infinite Creator. Go forth rejoicing in the power and in the peace of the One Glorious Infinite Creator. Adonai.

Session 100,
November 29, 1982

RA: I am Ra. I greet you, my friends, in the love and in the light of the One Infinite Creator. We communicate now.

QUESTIONER: Could you first please give me the condition of the instrument?

RA: I am Ra. It is as previously stated with the exception of the vital-energy distortion, which leans more towards strength/weakness than the last asking.

QUESTIONER: Thank you. To continue with the Tarot, I would like to make the additional observation with respect to Card Number Six that with the male's arms being crossed, if the female to his right pulls on his left hand it would turn his entire body, and the same is true for the female on the left pulling on his right hand from the other side. This is my interpretation of what is meant by the tangle of the arms. The transformation, then, occurs by the pull, which tends to turn the entity toward the left- or the right-hand path. Would Ra comment on that observation?

RA: I am Ra. We shall. The concept of the pull towards mental polarity may well be examined in the light of what the student has already accreted concerning the nature of the conscious, exemplified by the male, and the unconscious, exemplified by the female. Indeed, both the prostituted and the virginal of deep mind invite and await the reaching.

In this image of Transformation of Mind, then, each of the females points the way it would go, but is not able to move, nor are the two female entities striving to do so. They are at rest. The conscious entity holds both and will turn itself one way or the other or, potentially, backwards and forwards, rocking first one way then the other and not achieving the transformation. In order for the Transformation of Mind to occur, one principle governing the use of the deep mind must be abandoned.

It is to be noted that the triangular shape formed by the shoulders and crossed elbows of consciousness is a shape to be associated with transformation. Indeed, you may see this shape echoed twice more in the image, each echo having its own riches to add to the impact of this complex of concepts.

QUESTIONER: Thank you. We will probably return to this card in the next session with more observations after we consider Ra's comments. To make efficient use of our time, at this time I will make some notes with respect to Card Seven.

First, the veil between the conscious and unconscious mind is removed. The veil, I assume, is the curtain at the top and is lifted. Even though this veil has been removed, the perception of intelligent infinity is still distorted by the beliefs and means of seeking of the seeker. Would Ra comment on that?

RA: I am Ra. As one observes the veil of the image of the Great Way of Mind, it may be helpful to ideate using the framework of environment. The Great Way of Mind, Body, or Spirit is intended to limn the milieu within which the work of mind, body, or spirit shall be placed.

Thusly, the veil is shown both somewhat lifted and still present, since the work of mind and its transformation involves progressive lifting of the great veil betwixt the conscious and deep minds. The complete success of this attempt is not properly a portion of third-density work and, more especially, third-density mental processes.

QUESTIONER: The fact that the veil is raised higher on the right-hand side indicates to me that the adept choosing the positive polarity would have greater success in penetrating the veil. Would Ra comment?

RA: I am Ra. This is a true statement if it is realized that the questioner speaks of potential success. Indeed, your third-density experience is distorted or skewed so that the positive orientation has more aid than the so-called negative.

QUESTIONER: It would also seem to me that since Ra stated in the last session that the limit of the viewpoint is the source of all distortions,[9] the very nature of the service-to-self distortions that create the left-hand path are a function of the veil. Therefore, they are dependent, you might say, to some degree on at least a partial continued veiling. Does this make any sense?

9. Ra made this statement in response to a personal question, which, along with its answer, was removed from the last session.

RA: I am Ra. There is the thread of logic in what you suppose. The polarities are both dependent upon a limited viewpoint. However, the negative polarity depends more heavily upon the illusory separation betwixt the self and all other mind/body/spirit complexes. The positive polarity attempts to see through the illusion to the Creator in each mind/body/spirit complex but for the greater part is concerned with behaviors and thoughts directed towards other-selves in order to be of service. This attitude, in itself, is full of the stuff of your third-density illusion.

QUESTIONER: The crown of three stars, we are guessing, would represent the balancing of the mind, body, and spirit. Is this in any way correct?

RA: I am Ra. This device is astrological in origin, and the interpretation given somewhat confusing. We deal, in this image, with the environment of mind. It is perhaps appropriate to release the starry crown from its stricture.

QUESTIONER: The small black—or russet—and white entities have changed so that they now appear to be sphinxes, which we are assuming means that the catalyst has been mastered. I am also assuming that they act as the power that moves the chariot depicted here, so this mastery enables the mind in its transformation to become mobile, unlike it was prior to this mastery, locked as it was within the illusion. Would Ra comment?

RA: I am Ra. Firstly, we ask that the student consider the Great Way not as the culmination of a series of seven activities or functions but as a far more clearly delineated image of the environment within which the mind, body, or spirit shall function. Therefore, the culturally determined creatures called sphinxes do not indicate mastery over catalyst.

The second supposition, that of placing the creatures as the movers of the chariot of mind, has far more virtue. You may connote the concept of time to the image of the sphinx. The mental and mental/emotional complex ripens and moves and is transformed in time.

QUESTIONER: There is the forty-five-minute signal. Does Ra suggest a termination of this session, taking into consideration the instrument's condition?

RA: I am Ra. Information pertinent to this query has been previously covered. The choice of termination time, as you call it, is solely that of the questioner until the point at which we perceive the instrument beginning to use its vital resources due to the absence of transferred or native physical energy. The instrument remains open, as always.

QUESTIONER: In that case I will ask only one more question, and that will have to do with the sword and the scepter. It seems that the sword would represent the power of the negative adept in controlling other-selves, and the scepter would indicate the power of the positive adept operating in the unity of the mind, body, and spirit. However, they seem to be in the opposite hands than I would have guessed. Would Ra comment on these observations?

RA: I am Ra. These symbols are astrological in origin. The shapes, therefore, may be released from their stricture.

We may note that there is an overriding spiritual environment and protection for the environment of the mind. We may further note that the negatively polarized adept will attempt to fashion that covenant for its own use, whereas the positively polarized entity may hold forth that which is exemplified by the astrological sword; that is, light and truth.

QUESTIONER: Would there be two more appropriate objects or symbols to have the entity in Card Seven holding other than the ones shown?

RA: I am Ra. We leave this consideration to you, O student, and shall comment upon any observation which you may make.

QUESTIONER: Is there anything that we can do to make the instrument more comfortable or to improve the contact?

RA: I am Ra. All is well. The appurtenances are most conscientiously placed. We thank this diligent group. There is much-greater distortion towards harmony at this asking, and we join you in praise and thanksgiving. This is always the greatest boon to improvement of the contact, for it is the harmony of the group which supports this contact.

I am Ra. I leave you in the love and the light of the One. Go forth, therefore, rejoicing in the power and in the peace of the One Infinite Creator. Adonai.

Session 101, December 21, 1982, and Session 102, April 22, 1983, contain only personal material—pertaining to the illnesses of the instrument and the scribe which delayed the Ra contact during the winter—and were, for that reason, removed.

Session 103,
June 10, 1983

RA: I am Ra. I greet you in the love and in the light of the One Infinite Creator. We communicate now.

QUESTIONER: Could you first please give me the condition of the instrument?

RA: I am Ra. The physical distortions of the instrument remain serious. Further, the vital energies of this mind/body/spirit complex are much diminished, although acceptable for the needs of this working. This is to be noted as the lowest or most distorted vital reading of this all-important energy. The mental and mental/emotional distortions are as last seen.

We find the will of the instrument, having been unwisely used, to have encouraged the distortions of vital energy. It is well that the instrument ponder this.

QUESTIONER: What is the situation with respect to the physical problems with the digestive portions of the body that the instrument had previously?

RA: The yellow ray—we must correct ourselves. I am Ra. Please expel breath across this instrument's chest area.

[This was done as directed.]

RA: I am Ra. The channel is now satisfactory. We find the yellow-ray, chemical body of the instrument to be exhausted, but to be attempting the improvement by action such as exercise and diet. We may state that the infection has not completely left the body complex, although it is far less virulent.

QUESTIONER: What is the present situation with respect to our fifth-density, service-to-self-oriented companion?

RA: I am Ra. This entity has, for some period of your space/time, been at rest. However, it has been alerted to the workings taking place, and is soon to be your companion once again.

QUESTIONER: Can Ra recommend anything that the instrument can do, or that we can do, to improve any of the energies of the instrument?

RA: I am Ra. This is previously covered material. We have outlined the path the instrument may take in thought.

QUESTIONER: I didn't mean to cover previously covered material. I was hoping to add to this anything that we could do to specifically focus on at this time, the best possible thing that we or the instrument could do to improve these energies, the salient activity.

RA: I am Ra. Before responding, we ask your vigilance during pain flares, as the channel is acceptable but is being distorted periodically by the severe physical distortions of the yellow-ray, chemical body of the instrument.

Those salient items for the support group are praise and thanksgiving in harmony. These the group has accomplished with such a degree of acceptability that we cavil not at the harmony of the group.

As to the instrument, the journey from worth in action to worth in *esse* is arduous. The entity has denied itself in order to be free of that which it calls addiction.[10] This sort of martyrdom, and here we speak of the small but symbolically great sacrifice of the clothing, causes the entity to frame a selfhood in poorness, which feeds unworthiness unless the poverty is seen to be true richness. In other words, good works for the wrong reasons cause confusion and distortion. We encourage the instrument to value itself and to see that its true requirements are valued by the self. We suggest contemplation of true richness of being.

QUESTIONER: Is there anything else that either we or the instrument could do that would specifically work on the vital energy of the instrument to increase it?

---

10. The instrument made a New Year's resolution to give up buying clothes for herself for one year.

RA: I am Ra. We have come up against the full stop of free will.

QUESTIONER: In that case, I have a few questions on Card Number Seven in order to finish off our first run-through of the archetypes of the mind. There is a T with two right angles above it on the chest of the entity on Card Seven. We have guessed that the lower T has to do with the possibility of choosing either path in the transformation, and the upper two angles represent the great way of the left and the right-hand paths in the mental transformation that makes the change from space/time into time/space, you might say. This is difficult to express. Is anything correct in this?

RA: I am Ra. Yes.

QUESTIONER: Would Ra comment on that?

RA: I am Ra. The use of the tau[11] and the architect's square is indeed intended to suggest the proximity of the space/time of the Great Way's environment to time/space. We find this observation most perceptive.

The entire mood, shall we say, of the Great Way is indeed dependent upon its notable difference from the Significator. The Significator is the significant self, to a great extent but not entirely influenced by the lowering of the veil.

The Great Way of the Mind, the Body, or the Spirit draws the environment which has been the new architecture caused by the veiling process and, thusly, dipped in the great, limitless current of time/space.

QUESTIONER: I am guessing that the wheels of this chariot indicate the ability of the mind to be able to move in time/space. Is this correct?

RA: I am Ra. We cannot say that the observation is totally incorrect, for there is as much work in time/space as the individual who evokes this complex of concepts has assimilated.

However, it would be more appropriate to draw the attention to the fact that although the chariot is wheeled, it is not harnessed to that which draws it by a physical or visible harness. What then, O Student, links and harnesses the chariot's power of movement to the chariot?

QUESTIONER: I'll have to think about that. I'll come back to that.

---

11. tau: in heraldry, a type of cross called a "tau cross."

We were thinking of replacing the sword in the right hand with the magical sphere and putting a downward-pointing scepter in the left hand, similar to Card Five, the Significator, as symbols more appropriate for this card. Would Ra comment on that, please?

RA: I am Ra. This is quite acceptable, especially if the sphere may be imaged as spherical and effulgent.

QUESTIONER: The bent left leg of the sphinxes indicates a transformation that occurs on the left that doesn't occur on the right, possibly an inability in that position to move. Does this have any merit?

RA: I am Ra. The observation has merit in that it may serve as the obverse of the connotation intended. The position is intended to show two items, one of which is the dual possibilities of the timeful characters there drawn.

The resting is possible in time, as is the progress. If a mixture is attempted, the upright, moving leg will be greatly hampered by the leg that is bent. The other meaning has to do with the same right angle, with its architectural squareness, as the device upon the breast of the actor.

Time/space is close in this concept complex, brought close due to the veiling process and its efficaciousness in producing actors who wish to use the resources of the mind in order to evolve.

QUESTIONER: I am assuming that the skirt is skewed to the left for the same reason that it is in Card Number Four, indicating the distance service-to-self polarized entities keep from others, and I am also assuming that the face is turned to the left for the same reason that it is in Card Number Five, because of the nature of catalyst. Is this roughly correct?

RA: I am Ra. Please expel breath over the breast of the instrument from right to left.

[This was done as directed.]

I am Ra. That is well.

Your previous supposition is indeed roughly correct. We might also note that we, in forming the original images for your peoples, were using the cultural commonplaces of artistic expression of those in Egypt. The face is drawn to the side most often, as are the feet turned. We made use of this and, thus, wish to soften the significance of the sidelong look. In no case thus far in these deliberations, however, has any misinterpretation or unsuitable interpretation been drawn.

QUESTIONER: Our appropriate time limit for this working, I believe, is rapidly approaching, so I would like to ask what was the problem in this session when twice in this session we had to expel breath over the instrument's chest?

RA: I am Ra. This instrument is unaware of the method used to contact Ra. However, its desire was particularly strong, at the outset of this working, for this working to transpire. Thus it inadvertently was somewhat premature in its leaving of the yellow-ray, physical body.

In this state the object was dropped upon the instrument which you call the tie-pin microphone. The unexpected contact caused injury of the chest muscles, and we would advise some care depending from this working to avoid stress so that this injury may heal. There is a metaphysical component to this injury, and, therefore, we wished to be quite sure that all portions of the environment were cleansed. Since this place of working has not its usual level of protection, we used your breath to so cleanse the environment, which was at risk.

QUESTIONER: Is the reason for this lack of protection the fact that it has been a considerable time since we have worked in here?

RA: I am Ra. No.

QUESTIONER: What is the reason?

RA: I am Ra. The lack of regular repetition of the so-called Banishing Ritual is the lack of which we spoke.

QUESTIONER: From this I assume that it would be most appropriate to perform the Banishing Ritual daily in this room. Is this correct?

RA: I am Ra. That is acceptable.

QUESTIONER: I don't want to overtire the instrument. We're running close to time here. I will just ask if there is anything that we can do to improve the contact or to make the instrument more comfortable, and anything else that Ra could state at this time that would aid us?

RA: I am Ra. We find the alignments quite fastidiously observed. You are conscientious. Continue in support, one for the other, and find the praise and thanksgiving that harmony produces. Rest your cares and be merry.

I am Ra. I leave you, glorying in the love and in the light of the One Infinite Creator. Go forth, therefore, rejoicing in the power and in the peace of the One Infinite Creator. Adonai.

NOTE TO OUR READERS: As we look back over the material in Book IV, we find the following statement by Ra from Session 97 to be the key for this beginning of the study of the archetypical mind.

"We wish not to form that which may be considered by any mind/body/spirit complex to be a complete and infallible series of images. There is a substantial point to be made in this regard. We have been, with the questioner's aid, investigating the concept complexes of the great architecture of the archetypical mind. To more clearly grasp the nature, the process, and the purpose of archetypes, Ra provided a series of concept complexes. In no way whatsoever should we, as humble messengers of the One Infinite Creator, wish to place before the consideration of any mind/body/spirit complex, which seeks its evolution, the palest tint of the idea that these images are anything but a resource for working in the area of the development of the faith and the will.

To put this into perspective, we must gaze then at the stunning mystery of the One Infinite Creator. The archetypical mind does not resolve any paradoxes or bring all into unity. This is not the property of any source which is of the third density. Therefore, may we ask the student to look up from inward working and behold the glory, the might, the majesty, the mystery, and the peace of oneness. Let no consideration of bird or beast, darkness or light, shape or shadow, keep any which seeks from the central consideration of unity.

We are not messengers of the complex. We bring the message of unity. In this perspective only may we affirm the value to the seeker of adepthood of the grasping, articulating, and use of this resource of the deep mind exemplified by the concept complex of the archetypes."

EPILOGUE

After 106 sessions, the Ra contact ended with Don Elkin's death on November 7, 1984, after a year of declining health. It was the harmony between the three of us that supported the Ra contact; thus we no longer work with Ra or the trance state but now channel other Confederation sources. If you are interested in our other books, channeling transcripts, interviews, speeches, and more, please visit our archive website at www.llresearch.org. You may reach us by email at contact@llresearch.org or by "snail-mail" at L/L Research, PO Box 5195, Louisville, KY 40255-0195.

INDEX

ABOUT THE AUTHORS

DON ELKINS was born in Louisville, Kentucky, in 1930. He held a BS and MS in mechanical engineering from the University of Louisville, as well as an MS in general engineering from Speed Scientific School. He was professor of physics and engineering at the University of Louisville for twelve years from 1953 to 1965. In 1965 he left his tenured position and became a Boeing 727 pilot for a major airline to devote himself more fully to UFO and paranormal research. He also served with distinction in the US Army as a master sergeant during the Korean War.

Don Elkins began his research into the paranormal in 1955. In 1962, Don started an experiment in channeling, using the protocols he had learned from a contactee group in Detroit, Michigan. That experiment blossomed into a channeling practice that led eventually to the Law of One material 19 years later. Don passed away on November 7, 1984.

CARLA L. RUECKERT (McCarty) was born in 1943 in Lake Forest, Illinois. She completed undergraduate studies in English literature at the University of Louisville in 1966 and earned her master's degree in library service in 1971.

Carla became partners with Don in 1968. In 1970, they formed L/L Research. In 1974, she began channeling and continued in that effort until she was stopped in 2011 by a spinal fusion surgery. During four of those thirty-seven years of channeling (1981–1984), Carla served as the instrument for the Law of One material.

In 1987, she married Jim McCarty, and together they continued the mission of L/L Research. Carla passed into larger life on April 1, 2015.

JAMES MCCARTY was born in 1947 in Kearney, Nebraska. After receiving an undergraduate degrees from the University of Nebraska at Kearney and a master of science in early childhood education from the University of Florida, Jim moved to a piece of wilderness in Marion County, Kentucky, in 1974 to build his own log cabin in the woods, and to develop a self-sufficient lifestyle. For the next six years, he was in almost complete retreat.

He founded the Rock Creek Research and Development Laboratories in 1977 to further his teaching efforts. After experimenting, Jim decided that he preferred the methods and directions he had found in studying with L/L Research in 1978. In 1980, he joined his research with Don's and Carla's.

Jim and Carla were married in 1987. Jim has a wide L/L correspondence and creates wonderful gardens and stonework. He enjoys beauty, nature, dance, and silence.

NOTE: The Ra contact continued until session number 106. There are five volumes total in The Law of One series, Book I–Book V. There is also other material available from our research group on our archive website, www.llresearch.org.

You may reach us by email at contact@llresearch.org, or by mail at: L/L Research, P.O. Box 5195, Louisville, KY 40255–0195

MATRIX OF THE MIND
Arcanum Number I

THE MAGICIAN

POTENTIATOR OF THE MIND
Arcanum Number II

THE HIGH PRIESTESS

CATALYST OF THE MIND
Arcanum Number III

THE EMPRESS

EXPERIENCE OF THE MIND
Arcanum Number IV

THE EMPEROR

SIGNIFICATOR OF THE MIND
Arcanum Number V

THE HIEROPHANT

TRANSFORMATION OF THE MIND
Arcanum Number VI

THE TWO PATHS OR LOVERS

GREAT WAY OF THE MIND
Arcanum Number VII

THE CHARIOT OR CONQUEROR

NOTES

NOTES

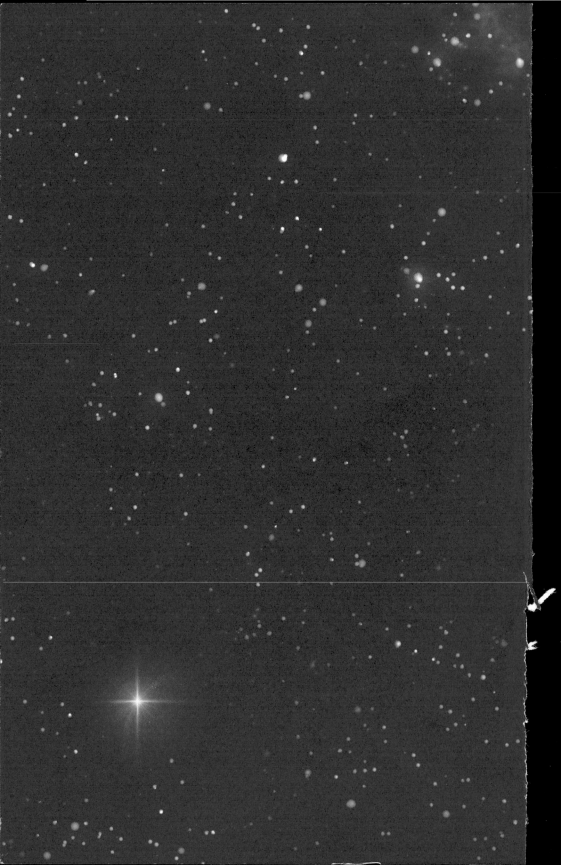